Risk in Banking

Maura La Torre

Risk in Banking

Developing a Knowledge Risk Management Framework for Cooperative Credit Banks

palgrave
macmillan

Maura La Torre
University "G. d'Annunzio"
of Chieti-Pescara
Pescara, Italy

ISBN 978-3-030-54497-3 ISBN 978-3-030-54498-0 (eBook)
https://doi.org/10.1007/978-3-030-54498-0

This Palgrave Pivot imprint is published by the registered company Springer Nature Switzerland AG
The registered company address is: Gewerbestrasse 11, 6330 Cham, Switzerland

Preface

Writing this book allowed me to merge my theoretical knowledge with reflections on real world challenges. My studies led me to have a mainly technical background. I approached financial system by analyzing its elements and interrelationships within it and toward the external environment. I have considered banks as the place of exchanging financial resources, the place where financial needs of the various operators of the economic system are met.

Subsequently, I broadened my vision, considering banks also as social organizations, and no longer just immaterial brokerage places. By studying authors such as Peter Massingham and Susanne Durst, I understood the usefulness of overcoming technicalities and paying more attention to the human aspect of these organizations, finding that behind every financial operation, there are people who create and exchange knowledge, or waste it, or lose it, or hide it, or forget it or even unlearn it. I understood, therefore, that knowledge could generate risks just as a financing operation can do; a particular type of risk, the knowledge risks. Analyzing contributions on this field, I was surprised by the effort to find studies specifically dedicated to banks and other financial institutions, although risk culture is deeply rooted in this organizations. The idea of this study came precisely from this observation, and from the intention to contribute to the development of an interesting and promising strand such as Knowledge Risk Management (KRM).

For these reasons, this book has the dual purpose of answer the call for more research on Knowledge Risk Management (KRM), and propose the first KRM framework specific for banks, in particular, for cooperative credit banks (CCBs).

I chose the Italian Cooperative Credit Banks as sample of my analysis, because currently these banks are facing the challenges of a reform that leads them to being at same time local banks and parts of a banking group; a challenging situation both from a knowledge management and risk management point of view.

I like to think of this Book as a "pilot study", which will hopefully promote new contributions involving different types of banks and other financial institutions, and aiming to constitute an independent line of research.

For this reason, instead of saying what could be learned from this book, I prefer to say what I learned by writing it.

I learned that there is still a lot to write about knowledge risks and a lot more to share; I learned that knowledge management and risk management are still "separate worlds" in organizations belonging to banking and financial sectors; I learned that Italian cooperative banks need a structured approach to Knowledge Risk Management to better deal with the changes they are facing with. I learned that there is still much to learn in this field.

In any case, I hope this book will be at least a starting point to encourage readers to further exploration of the proposed themes.

Pescara, Italy

Acknowledgments

I want to thank several special people who helped me in the project of this book. First of all, I would like to thank Dr. Peter Massingham, who has put his vast experience in the field of Knowledge Management and Knowldge risk management at my disposal. Special thanks to Dr. Ermanno Alfonsi and Professor Michele Samuele Borgia, who by believing in this project, made possible the involvement of the Federation of CCBs in this research. I also wish to thank the editorial team at Palgrave Macmillan, especially Tula Weis and Ashwini Elango for their support in this work.

Contents

About the Author

Maura La Torre received two Ph.D. *cum laude* in "Management of Innovation" and in "Economics and Management of Natural Resources" at University "G. d'Annunzio", of Chieti-Pescara, Italy, and at University LUM Jean Monnet, Casamassima, Bari, Italy. She is currently postdoctoral fellow at Department of Management and Business Administration, University "G. d'Annunzio", of Chieti-Pescara.

List of Figures

List of Tables

CHAPTER 1

Introduction

Abstract This chapter introduces the aim of the book, synthetically considering the motivations for which a study on Knowledge Risk management in banks could be timely and useful both from a theoretical and a practical point of view. Moreover, the chapter presents the structure of the book, summarizing the main topics covered in each Chapter.

Keywords Knowledge Risk Management · Banks · Structure of the book

This book has a dual purpose, to answer the call for more research on Knowledge Risk Management (KRM), and to propose a KRM framework specific for banks, in particular, for cooperative credit banks (CCBs).

The choice to deal with KRM is not connected only with the interest in a strand still in its infancy, but it comes, above all, from the fact that, surprisingly, in banking and finance research, so far, KRM and its related topics have been just marginally addressed.

Although KRM is still a developing strand, interest in this field is growing in recent years, and more and more scholars are approaching it, providing valuable learning opportunities (Bratianu, 2018; Durst & Henschel, 2020; Durst & Zięba, 2017, 2018; Massingham, 2008, 2010). Nonetheless, attention to KRM by scholars involved in finance and banking studies seems to be still limited. This really surprises, at least

M. La Torre, *Risk in Banking*,
https://doi.org/10.1007/978-3-030-54498-0_1

the author of this book, since practically all organizations belonging to financial and banking sectors are exposed to several risks in carrying out their typical activities. Banks, for example, face different types of risk: credit risk, liquidity risk, market risks, or operational risk. Why not also knowledge risks? It is precisely from this question that the present study moves.

Knowledge risk has been defined as a "measure of the probability and severity of adverse effects of any activities engaging or related somehow to the knowledge that can affect the functioning of an organization on any level" (Durst & Zięba, 2018, p. 2). Therefore, each organization could be exposed to different knowledge risks. Even banks and other financial institutions. And this is why scholars and practitioners have started to deal more and more with KRM issues, so as to be able to provide management with tools and techniques for their control and mitigation. The same would be expected from banking and finance research, but the state-of-the-art of literature currently shows a shortage of contributions specifically dealing with knowledge risks management in organizations belonging to these sectors. This work, therefore, appears to be timely and necessary, even more because it is focused on a particular type of banks, i.e., cooperative credit banks.

The post-financial crisis scenario put European cooperative banks facing complex challenges. The exceptionally low level of interest rates set by the European Central Bank, the low profitability of traditional banking services—the real sustenance of cooperative banking—as well as the entry of Fintech companies into financial markets, put cooperative banking sector under pressure, making more difficult for CCBs to preserve the unique and distinctive characteristics of their business model (Migliorelli, 2018). In the case of Italian cooperative banks, the situation was further complicated by a reform based on the establishment of Cooperative Banking Groups—a completely new figure in the Italian and European banking sectors—to which cooperative banks are obliged to adhere. These organizational transformations required Italian cooperative banks to make an additional effort to maintain their characteristics of local banks, despite having to be part of a wider and more complex reality such as a banking group. In this situation, a governance capable of facing unprecedented challenges, and an effective risk management able to face an increasing number of risks became of crucial importance for Italian cooperative banks. On the basis of these premises, we considered CCBs the ideal sample for the present research, being currently engaged in strong organizational changes that also entail having to manage new and more complex knowledge. Investigating, therefore, the presence or absence of awareness of a risky side of knowledge, potentially harmful to the bank, seemed to satisfy the dual purpose of this book, that is to contribute to development of KRM strand—providing the experience of a type of organization little covered in literature—and to propose a framework for knowledge risks management specific for banks.

In order to achieve the above-mentioned, this book consists of six chapters. This introduction will be followed by Chapter 2, which provides an overview of the main concept of Knowledge Management, Risk Management, and Knowledge Risk Management, in order to provide basic information on these issues also to the reader more specialized in banking and finance. A focus on knowledge risks is provided as well, including an explanation of their main characteristics and potential harmfulness. Chapter 3 is aimed at verify the shortage of research contributions on Knowledge Risk Management with specific reference to organizations belonging to financial and banking sectors, performing a systematic review. To contextualize this review, recent trends in knowledge management in banks and other financial firms are also provided, and some aspects of strengths and weaknesses of today's risk management of these organizations are considered as well. Chapter 4 includes insights into the sample of cooperative banks involved in the analysis conducted in this book, i.e., the CCBs members of the *Federazione delle Banche di Credito Cooperativo dell'Abruzzo e del Molise (Fedam).* To better understand the challenging changes these banks are actually facing, an overview of the Italian Cooperative System is provided; direct experience of an administrator of a CCbs member of Fedam is also presented to obtain further information from the real operations of a cooperative bank every day at the forefront of the fight against risks, including knowledge risks. In Chapter 4, a section dedicated to diversity in baking as a strength/weakness of cooperative banks is also included.

The readiness of cooperative credit banks in Knowledge Risk Management is addressed in Chapter 5, performing a case study on a sample of Italian cooperative credit banks. Considering the results of this analysis, a KRM framework specific for cooperative credit banks is proposed.

The book ends with Chapter 6 dedicated to concluding remarks and suggestions for further future research.

References

Bratianu, C. (2018). A holistic approach to knowledge risk. *Management Dynamics in the Knowledge Economy, 6*(4), 593–607.

Durst, S., & Henschel, T. (2020). *Knowledge risk management: From theory to praxis*. Berlin: Springer.

Durst, S., & Zięba, M. (2017). Knowledge risks—Towards a taxonomy. *International Journal of Business Environment, 9*(1), 51–63.

Durst, S., & Zięba, M. (2018). Mapping knowledge risks: Towards a better understanding of knowledge management. *Knowledge Management Research & Practice, 17*(1), 1–13.

Massingham, P. (2008). Measuring the impact of knowledge loss: More than ripples on a pond? *Management Learning, 39*(5), 541–560.

Massingham, P. (2010). Knowledge risk management: A framework. *Journal of Knowledge Management, 14*(3), 464–485.

Migliorelli, M. (2018). Cooperative banks lending during and after the Great Crisis. In *New cooperative banking in Europe* (pp. 47–85). Cham: Palgrave Macmillan.

CHAPTER 2

When Knowledge Becomes Risky … and Other Stories

Abstract The aim of this chapter is to provide a frame of the main topics related to knowledge, Knowledge Management (KM) and Knowledge Risk Management (KRM), considering the contribution of some of the most leading scholars to these strands. Throughout this chapter, readers will obtain an overview of some relevant terms and concepts, which could serve as background in addressing topics covered by the other chapters of this book. In particular, the importance of knowledge, especially the tacit and skilful ones, is highlighted, as well as the "dark side" of knowledge and its harmfulness for organizations are considered; up to also analyzing the set of tools and techniques to manage the risks associated with knowledge's use, namely Knowledge Risk Management (KRM). Moreover, a digression on the main types of knowledge risks is provided as well. For each knowledge risk, information will be provided about their main characteristics, the potential harmfulness, and how (or if) they are included in organizations' risk management.

Keywords Knowledge Management · Knowledge Risk Management · Knowledge risks · Skilful knowing

M. La Torre, *Risk in Banking*,
https://doi.org/10.1007/978-3-030-54498-0_2

2.1 Introduction

In this book, the application of tools and techniques typical of Knowledge Management (KM) to the context of the banking sector is proposed. For this reason, it is important to provide readers with an overview of certain topics that can support them in addressing the contents of the other chapters of the book. In order to achieve the above-mentioned, in this chapter it will be a priority to highlight the importance of tacit knowledge and its relationship with explicit knowledge; as well as important it will be to consider risks potentially inherent in knowledge management, and roles and responsibilities within the organization in preventing these risks from becoming a concrete threat to corporate competitiveness. Besides, topics covered in this chapter are approached through the perspective of some of the most important scholars which, over the years, have dealt with knowledge, its management, and its potential to become risky.

In particular, in Sect. 2.2, given the importance of knowledge, especially tacit knowledge, the concept of skilful knowing and the identification of its potential against the harmfulness of knowledge loss are proposed. In Sect. 2.3, a dynamic view of Knowledge management also including its temporal perspective is addressed; while in Sect. 2.4 the concept of Knowledge Risk Management (KRM) is introduced starting from its definition, to then consider its theoretical perspective, the state of the art from the research point of view, to end with a discussion on knowledge risk management in practice. The chapter ends with the presentation of the most known knowledge risks identified and mapped so far; a sort of “identity card” is provided for these risks, containing information on each of the knowledge risks regarding the origin, main characteristics, the level of diffusion within the organizations, and their potential for harmfulness (Sect. 2.5).

2.2 When Knowledge Becomes Risky

Ever since Robert Grant (1996) and Peter Drucker (1988) referred to knowledge as the most valuable resource for organizations of any type and size, and as the main driver of economic value, a plethora of researchers and practitioners worldwide dealt with knowledge and its management. To date, the reference literature provides hundreds of knowledge definitions. In this book, one of the most recent of these definitions is proposed, according to which “knowledge is a highly valued state in which a person is in cognitive contact with reality. It is, therefore, a relation" (Zagzebski, 2017, p. 92). Considering knowledge as a relation allows a digression on the dualism tacit knowledge-explicit knowledge, which still today represents the key to understanding the process of knowledge creation in organizations. Tacit knowledge involves intangible factors such as personal beliefs, perspectives and the system of personal values and, interacting with explicit knowledge, contributes to the process of knowledge creation within the organizations. Considered in its cognitive dimension, tacit knowledge consists of "[...] schemata, mental models, beliefs, and perceptions so ingrained that we take them for granted. The cognitive dimension of tacit knowledge reflects our image of reality (what is) and our vision for the future (what ought to be) [...] these implicit models shape the way we perceive the world around us" (Nonaka & Takeuchi, 1995, p. 21). Explicit knowledge can be articulated in "formal language, mathematical expressions, specifications, manuals and so forth; is a kind of knowledge that can be transmitted across individuals formally and easily" (Nonaka & Takeuchi, 1995, p. 7). Historically, there has always been a kind of tension between explicit and tacit knowledge, the same tension that exists between process and practice: "[...] process represents explicit knowledge, or how knowledge is organized; practice represents tacit knowledge, or the way work is really done" (Smith, 2001, p. 318). Only organizations that are able to mitigate this tension—finding a balance between these two types of knowledge—can benefit from their correct application: tacit knowledge, when the goal is the pursuit of creativity and innovation; explicit knowledge, on the other hand, one must trust in a precise and predictable organization of tasks and competences in the organization. In any case, the important thing is to act: "[...] human inertia is the single biggest obstacle to knowledge management efforts" (Wah, 2000, p. 147). In order for knowledge to be created, people need to activate processes of transferring and sharing what they know, and apply what they learn. But people often do not know what knowledge they are lacking: firms must intervene to highlight that there is something to know. Top managers must act as "guardians of knowledge," constantly probing the unknown and bouncing it from the teams of project to make them think of new ideas (Wah, 2000).

With respect to considerations made so far, it may be interesting to report an example contained in a work by Polanyi, a chemist turned philosopher, that was categorical on the fact that all knowing implies a skilful action, and that the knower necessarily participates in all the acts of understanding:

> Consider the use of geographical maps. A map represents a part of the earth's surface in the same sense in which experimental science represents a much greater variety of experience. To use a map to find our way, we must be able to do three things. First we must identify our actual position in the landscape with a point on the map, then we must find on the map an itinerary toward our destination, and, finally, we must identify this itinerary by various landmarks in the landscape around us. Thus map-reading Successful identification of actual locations with points on a map depends upon the good judgment of a skilled map-reader. No map can read itself. Neither can the most explicit possible treatise on map-reading read a map. (Polanyi & Prosch, 1975, p. 39)

From this example, it is clear that Polanyi categorically rejects the idea that exist a knowledge that is objective, autonomous, detached, and independent of human action: "[…] new knowledge comes about not when the tacit becomes explicit, but when our skilled performance is punctuated in new ways through social interaction" (Tsoukas, 2005, p. 123). Therefore, according to Polanyi, knowing involves "skilful action." Knowledge emerges in the act of doing something when people are fully aware of what they are doing, that is, they are aware of the knowledge needed to complete the activity. According to the theory of skilful knowing, work becomes an adaptive process in which the individual tries to transform given situations into preferred situations; problem solving is based on individual practice which goes beyond bureaucratic guidelines (Massingham, 2019a, p. 53–54).

The main purpose of skilful knowing is to ensure the availability of the knowledge necessary for the organization to creating value, reducing uncertainty, and managing risk. When knowledge is unavailable, it creates risk, as the organization is unable to perform these activities or not perform them at optimal levels. When knowledge is unavailable, it results knowledge loss (Massingham, 2019a). Knowledge loss can be considered today one of the most dangerous threats to organizations, because it has the direct result of the inevitable decrease in performance and profitability (Massingham, 2019a). The possibility for an organization to be exposed to the risk of knowledge loss becomes concrete, for example, in the case of employee exit organizations, lost codified knowledge, or knowledge decay (Massingham, 2019a, p. 208); this must make think about how easy it could be to suffer negative effects of knowledge loss, about how it is a trap that can hide in the normal practices of each organization.

All organizations, in daily operations, continually lose knowledge. According to DeLong (2004, p. 31), "the trick is figuring out beforehand, which knowledge—if it's lost—will undermine organisational strategy." The author also identified at least five main ways in which this could happen: (i) reduced ability to innovate; (ii) threatened ability to pursue growth strategies; (iii) reduced efficiency undermines low-cost strategies; (iv) losing consciousness can give an advantage to competitors; and (v) losing specific knowledge at the wrong time increases vulnerability.

That considered, skilful knowing could help our understanding of risk of knowledge loss for several reasons:

1. Organizational capability. Knowledge creates value for organizations through the performance of activities. Value emerges through innovation, problem solving, or creativity (Massingham, 2019a).
2. Uncertainty. The complexity of modern business generates high levels of uncertainty within the context of emergent effects that can escalate rapidly (Massingham, 2019b) Knowledge can make unknowns known (Massingham, 2019c).
3. Risk management. Subject matter experts manage risk for their organization (Massingham, 2010). Expert systems have emerged at the forefront of the modeling of problems (Akhavan, Shahabipour, & Hosnavi, 2018). Experts have the knowledge to properly assess risk and how best to manage it (Massingham, 2010).

Definitely, the possibility of finding effective solutions against knowledge loss depends on how much the damaging potential of this loss is known. In this sense, knowledge usage is a positive action when it prevents the waste of knowledge; in fact, unused knowledge is wasted knowledge: the difference between knowing what to do and not to do it, this gap represents wasted knowledge resources, a circumstance that could undermine the stability of organizations (Massingham, 2019a). While knowledge usage is a people's issue, it's a precise responsibility of the organization to help make this happen: "the correct use of knowledge implies learning from experience before, during and after activities. This temporal perspective allows us to learn from the past, improve the present and plan the future" (Massingham, 2019a, p. 26).

2.3 Knowledge Management: The Past, the Present, the Future

As anticipated at the beginning of this chapter, it is not in the intentions of this book's author to be exhaustive in dealing with such broad and debated issues as knowledge and knowledge management, but to grasp only what is the vision referred to among the many proposals over the years by different scholars. So, as for the knowledge definition, also for that of knowledge management our point of reference was the work of Peter Massingham (2019a, p. 64), who defined knowledge management as a "Theory for all organizations and every manager. Good organizations and managers should be interested in learning from experience, improving performance, and developing sustainable competitive advantage. This makes knowledge management accessible for everyone." The dynamic view of Knowledge management also included a temporal perspective of it. *"I believe that knowledge management tries to capture the past, improve on the present, and plan for the future."* With this statement, Massingham (2019a, p. 65) was one of the first to refer to a knowledge management perspective based on its triple time dimension:

1. Capture the past, learning from it, and applying what has been learned.
2. Present: manage the present by sharing knowledge efficiently and improving the way work is performed.
3. Future: plan for the future to create sustainable competitive advantage through the correct use of knowledge and its management.

One of the main practical purposes of knowledge management is to prevent knowledge drain (loss) by sharing explicit and tacit knowledge among employees (Lee et al., 2014, p. 384).

Massingham (2019a) pointed out that the knowledge loss problem has been addressed by several disciplines, including: knowledge management, human resource management, and operations management. From literature review of these disciplines, attempts to find solutions for the damage caused by knowledge loss in organizations emerged. In particular:

- The knowledge management (KM) literature: measuring the impact of knowledge loss and knowledge sharing as a method to prevent knowledge loss (e.g., see Massingham & Massingham, 2014).
- The human resource management (HRM) literature: employee retention strategies such as succession planning, policies to retain older workers or engage retirees, or building a retention culture including motivation and reward systems (e.g., see DeLong, 2004).
- The operations management (OM) literature: solutions by integrating the activities of the value chain (Closs, Jacobs, Swink, & Webb, 2008), on codification strategies including investments in information technology tools and systems (Rothenburger & Galarreta, 2006), and on standard operating procedures (SOPs) (Han & Park, 2009).
- Risk management (RM) literature: risk management strategies and risk mitigation initiatives are "best developed and managed where the risk exposure occurs" (Kallenberg, 2009, p. 93). This discussion emphasizes the risk of knowledge loss if risk managers exit the organization or are otherwise unavailable, e.g., on leave or deployed elsewhere. A challenge for expert system designers is to develop a knowledge management system that includes a "meaningful model of uncertainty associated with complex models" (Akhavan et al., 2018, p. 424). Uncertainty modeling is widely used in systems analysis (Akhavan et al., 2018, p. 424). Akhavan et al. (2018, p. 425) argues that "the aim of risk management is to reduce uncertainty by envisioning possible scenarios and making forecasts on the basis of what itis considered probable within a range of possibilities." The reduction of uncertainty associated with knowledge loss necessary to manage risk is a complex challenge.

2.4 Knowledge Risk Management: Not Only Knowledge Assets but Also Liabilities

2.4.1 Defining Knowledge Risk Management

Knowledge risk management (KRM) emerged in 2010 offering a solution to the problems associated with conventional risk management methods (Massingham, 2010). KRM uses "knowledge management tools and techniques to enable individuals to generate deeper insight about the real nature of organizational risk" (Massingham, 2010, p. 465). KRM is novel theory that adopts a "more pragmatic multi-disciplinary mixed methods approach from management science" to solve problems otherwise "intractable" for conventional views on risk management (Ilina & Vargab, 2015, p. 241). KRM's novelty is how it provides a completely new insightful line of thinking by using concepts from operational, organizational, and behavioral research to model "the complex phenomena of systemic risk in its social contexts" (Ilina & Vargab, 2015, p. 241). The multi-disciplinary concepts are explained further in the sections on theoretical perspectives and measurement which follow.

KRM is therefore an interesting line of research, which can involve different disciplines and operational contexts. Nevertheless, some scholars pointed that research on knowledge risks is still in a phase of incomplete maturity (Durst, 2019; Massingham, 2010, 2018). Given the strategic importance of knowledge and its "relevance for organizational development and sustainability" (Durst, 2019, p. 26), it seems unwise to underestimate impact of knowledge risks. Durst (2019) argues that KRM is essential to ensure knowledge strategies and management are effective (Durst, 2019, p. 26): at a practical level, KRM addresses the weaknesses in the traditional normative probabilistic decision tree model of risk management. It focuses on expert knowledge and, therefore extends operations risk management by providing a structured process for understanding and using experts' experience, as well as the risks posed if this knowledge is lost (Massingham, 2010).

2.4.2 Theoretical Perspectives on Knowledge Risk Management

Knowledge risk management (KRM) has theoretical foundations across multiple disciplines. There are several important themes. First, is complexity theory. Complexity theory deals with the dynamic nonlinear behavior of systems (Fisser & Browaeys, 2010). Complexity theory provides an "integrative and dynamic framework to understand the interaction patterns in networks of interdependent agents who interact and are bound by their common needs or objectives" (Borzillo & Kaminska-Labbe, 2011, p. 356). Complexity thinking lies somewhere between a belief in a "fixed and fully knowable universe" and "a fear that meaning and reality are so dynamic" that their discovery is delusional (Davis & Sumara, 2006, p. 4). The former is normative probabilistic decision tree models of risk management, while the latter is chaos theory. Complexity is not chaos. Chaos theory cannot explain the "structure, the coherence, the self-organizing cohesiveness of complex systems" (Waldrop, 1992, p. 12). Complex systems are organised by their self-regulation and adaptability (Massingham, 2019d). KRM aims to provide self-regulation and adaptability to the complexity posed by risk via the expert social systems. Complexity emerges in the problem of environmental complexity manifested by individuals not knowing enough about the risk to anticipate its likelihood and consequences (Massingham, 2010). Environmental complexity creates uncertainty. Knowledge moves individuals along the spectrum of uncertainty toward certainty; making risk a "learnable" rather than an entirely random event (Massingham, 2010). Recent research examines how knowledge, represented as collective social intelligence, may reduce uncertainty associated with solving complex problems (Massingham, 2019d).

Second, is strategic management theory. The late 1980s saw the emergence of the resource-based view of the firm (RBV) and, soon after, the knowledge-based view (KBV) of the firm (KBV). These theories explained that knowledge was a firm resource and that it could be combined with other resources, such as technology, capital, and materials, to create value for the firm via organizational capabilities. The KBV made knowledge matter (Massingham, 2019a). The resource-based view provides the following concepts for knowledge strategy: knowledge has value, it meets the criteria for sustainable competitive advantage, and it creates competitive advantage with the know-how to combine other resources into capabilities see Massingham, 2019a). The KBV regards the organization as an institution for generating and applying knowledge (Grant, 1996). The KBV explains that knowledge management is not about technology or its discipline information science; rather, it is about people and their knowledge, and that has been and always will be a challenge. The risks associated by the KBV are found in the coordination and cooperation problems. The coordination problem is "how to integrate the separate efforts of multiple individuals who may have varying levels of motivation and capacity to interact" (Grant, 2002, p. 136). The KBV argues that the challenges for management are to "establish the mechanisms by which cooperating individuals can coordinate their activities in order to integrate their knowledge into productive activity" (Grant, 1997, p. 452). This creates risks in the trade-off decision between being an expert against the time it takes to engage with others.

Third, is knowledge management. Knowledge loss is increasing due to workforce mobility and our ageing society. Massingham (2019a) recently explored why knowledge loss matters and how to address it. His model of knowledge loss examined the likelihood and consequences of knowledge loss from multiple perspectives and added a temporal dimension. The model considers what happens after knowledge loss at the individual level, i.e., the remaining employees, and at the organizational level in terms of performance (Massingham, 2019a). Massingham (2019a) discusses how to manage knowledge loss from various perspectives.

These three themes—complexity theory, strategic management theory, and knowledge management theory—illustrated the multi-disciplinary approach to knowledge risk and its management. In summary, knowledge risk management requires understanding uncertainty (complexity theory); understanding impact, designing solutions, and prioritizing for action (strategic management theory); and understanding the role of knowledge in providing solutions, as well as the risks posed by not having this knowledge, and how to manage it (knowledge management theory).

2.4.3 Research on Knowledge Risks Management: The State of the Art

"The Management of Knowledge Risks: What Do We Really Know?" With this question, Durst, Bruns, and Henschel (2018) well interpreted the state of the art of research on knowledge risks and their management. Compared to the multitude of theoretical and empirical studies that over the decades implemented the research on Knowledge Management and Risk Management, literature on Knowledge Risk Management still appears to be lacking in its definitive autonomy and organization. This situation could largely depend on the fact that, for a long time, scholars dealt more with the "bright side" of organizations, focusing their studies mainly on excellence, and tending to overlook business decline or failure (Stam, 2009). Therefore, knowledge is hardly ever associated with organizational decay, since it is usually considered rather a solution. Always Durst, Bruns, and Henschel (2018, p. 260) argued that organizations, regardless of type and size, may run into some situations in which the application of knowledge, or its lack, could expose them to a number of risks related to this resource. Specifically, they referred to: (a) risks related to human resources, deriving from the normal turnover or prolonged absence of founders, managers, and staff; (b) relational risk, which mainly result from ineffective and inefficient relationships that the organization establishes with partners, or from opportunistic behaviors of the latter; (c) risks related to the decision-making process, when new strategies are implemented, or new markets are conquered with new products; (d) risks related to the existence of a gap between what the organization must know and what it actually knows, a circumstance that could make the achievement of corporate objectives complex; (e) risks associated with the outsourcing of corporate functions; and (f) risks related to the loss of such knowledge that had to remain within the organization.

The first significant contribution to know what is known so far about the management of knowledge risks always comes from Durst, Bruns, and Henschel (2018). The authors, starting from the observation that scientific production on knowledge risks is currently still in an incomplete stage of maturity—they reported that the oldest publication is from 2001, while the most recent from 2014, with an intensification of research only after 2012—organized the main literature on knowledge risk management into two strands. The first one including studies aimed to supporting organizations of different types in the mitigation of knowledge risks, by proposing specific frameworks and tools. Among these, Peter Massingham, proposed a method based on knowledge management constructs, which "provides manager with a way to differentiate among risks and prioritize for action. Its main value is to reduce the cognitive bias inherent in traditional decision methods for risk assessment" (Massingham, 2010, p. 464). Included in the second strand, instead, those studies focused on different phases of Knowledge Risk Management implementation: awareness, complexity, identification and classification, strategy, and protection.

The remaining part of the revised literature flowed into the sub-topic "Knowledge Risk Management practices."

The literature review performed by Durst, Bruns, and Henschel (2018) included research published until 2015. In a more recent contribution (Durst, 2019, p. 23), the KRM literature review revealed slightly different data: currently, there are researches up to 2018, with a special interest in the topic in the years 2012 and 2013. During and after 2018, studies based on the metaphor of knowledge as energy had also contributed to the implementation of Knowledge Risk Management strand, proposing a holistic approach including three further fields of knowledge: rational, emotional and spiritual; this approach, by associating the risk with each of these knowledge fields, gave the concept of knowledge risk greater breadth and complexity (Bratianu, 2018). The knowledge risk practices strand was also implemented with a recent contribution focused on different experiences with knowledge risks, in different sectors of the economy and in different types of organizations, including case studies on family firms, to those on State-Owned Companies (Durst & Henschel, 2020); while, in other studies, the relationship between KRM and organizational performance has been addressed, and the connection between business sustainability and knowledge risks has been considered as well (Durst, Hinteregger, & Zięba, 2019; Durst & Zięba, 2020).

All these efforts contributed to provide a clearer and more precise definition of Knowledge Risk Management (KRM), as a "systematic way of applying tools and techniques to identify, analyse and respond to risks associated with the creation, application and retention of organizational knowledge. Similar to knowledge management, KRM should have a long-term orientation and different KM practices can be expected to support continued risk management of an organization' s knowledge that is up to date and relevant" (Durst & Henschel, 2020, p. 7).

In a study on the importance of Knowledge Risk Management for SMEs, Durst and Ferenhof (2016) then outlined the phases of KRM process. In the first of these phases, identification of the risk took place, a phase in which the organization must become aware of the types of risk to which it could be exposed, considering both aspects related to the management of human resources (with their knowledge capital), and the management of knowledge in the various phases of organizational life (possibility of losing or wasting knowledge even in an unintentional way). This phase is followed by that of risk analysis, in which risks identified in the previous phase are studied and classified on the basis of their potential for harmfulness, and basing on the probability that they arise during the organizational life. Phase three focuses on the actual management of the risks identified and analyzed, developing and implementing risk mitigation strategies, monitoring the effectiveness of the measures taken and intervening where necessary to modify any weaknesses and inefficiencies. The KRM process ends with a phase of continued reporting on previous actions, so as to keep the identified risks under control, their threatening nature and the effectiveness of the measures taken to mitigate them.

2.4.4 Practicing Knowledge Risk Management

Massingham (2010, p. 465) initially proposed knowledge risk management as a decision support tool, i.e., conceptual model, to address the problem of cognitive constraints presented by conventional decision tree methods. KRM was a set of KM tools and techniques "to enable individuals to generate deeper insight about the real nature of organizational risk" (Massingham, 2010, p. 465). The essence of Massingham's (2010) thinking was the need for a paradigm switch away from the conventional focus on the risk event adopted by the normative probabilistic models, to a focus on the knowledge necessary to manage the risk event. This new paradigm addressed the cognitive constraints associated with the decision tree models, particularly in terms of personal bias and subjectivity. This change in thinking was achieved by focusing risk assessment and risk management on what people need to know rather than what people do. Massingham (2010) argued that the most serious risk was not having knowledge necessary to manage the risk available, e.g., through knowledge loss, rather than the risk event itself. The risk event could be managed if knowledge was available. If the knowledge is not available, the risk event's likelihood and consequences then becomes a very serious threat.

There have been only a few studies that have tried to explain knowledge risk management in practice. This research is limited to four studies that have quantitatively assessed and measured knowledge drain risk, i.e., knowledge loss (Jennex & Durcikova, 2013; Lee et al., 2014; Massingham, 2010, 2018). Jennex and Durcikova measured individual-level risk; Leet et al., examined social network-level risk; while Massingham's models look at the individual, the group, the organization, and the knowledge resource itself.

Jennex and Durcikova (2013) proposed an algorithm to evaluate the risk of losing knowledge by losing experts. This algorithm calculates the risk of knowledge loss by multiplying three variables: probability of knowledge loss, consequence of knowledge loss, and quality of the knowledge source. It provides a score from 1 to 10,000 calculating the risk of knowledge loss at the individual level. This is useful because it measures the risk of losing the knowledge of a particular expert. However, it is limited as it simply provides a score and a priority ranking in terms of risk, but does not consider the consequences of losing relationships in organizational networks.

Lee et al. (2014) used network analysis to identify an individual's influence in the network. The paper looks at the impact of knowledge loss on the social network under two scenarios: (1) when an exiting employee is a network leader and (2) when an exiting employee is an isolated expert (Lee et al., 2014, p. 383). This distinction is an important contribution to the field. By measuring the impact of losing experts at opposite ends of the social network spectrum—those with little interaction with others compared to influential members in the network with much interaction—the study situates the risks of knowledge loss within the context of others, i.e., those that remain the social network after the expert has left. Massingham extends this thinking in his Massingham (2018) paper. The Lee et al. (2014) study measured the impact associated with a specific individual in a social network (i.e., a Community of Practice), by considered network effect and knowledge quality. Network effect is highly related to knowledge loss associated with departures of network leaders, whereas knowledge quality category is associated with departures of isolated experts. Lee et al. (2014, p. 388) developed a metric to "quantitatively measure the existence and seriousness of potential loss."

Massingham (2010, 2018, 2019a) developed various models to quantify the level of knowledge management risk, as well as the solutions necessary to manage this risk. In summary, Massingham's knowledge risk management model measures the impact of lost knowledge about a risk event in three steps:

1. Calculation of the level of risk associated with each of the main activities of the organization, following the conventional method of the decision tree: the probability and consequences of an unwanted event that occurs, with the addition of a weighting based on the relative importance of each activity.
2. Calculation of the level of risk associated with the knowledge necessary to manage the risk factors for each activity.
3. Prioritization of risks for action by considering the outcomes of step 1 and step 2 in isolation and then in combination.

According to Massingham (2018, 2019a), knowledge risk is calculated involving three knowledge risk characteristics: individual, knowledge, and organizational, and their six constructs.

2.4.4.1 *Individual Characteristics*

1. Recruitment effectiveness. Defined as Necessary Qualification Levels (NQL), is determined by the organization's ability to attract suitably qualified staff, and is measured by the levels of pre-requisite knowledge (i.e., qualifications) necessary to manage the risk factor (i.e., the unwanted event). The higher the qualification levels, the more difficult it will be to recruit, and vice versa. "*The higher the qualifications, the greater the risk that human capital cannot be bought*" (Massingham, 2018, p. 743).
2. Training efficiency. Defined as Time To Learn (TTL), it is determined by the time required for staff training (human capital development). "*The more time required to learn, the greater the risk that human capital cannot be developed*" (Massingham, 2018, p. 743).

2.4.4.2 *Knowledge Characteristics*

1. Tacitness. Determined by the location of the knowledge needed to manage the risk factor, which is defined as Receiver Transfer Access (RTA), and is measured by the degree to which people who need knowledge can access it. If the knowledge needed to manage risk is found only in people's heads, i.e., tacit knowledge, the organization is vulnerable if not available. "*Alternatively, if the necessary knowledge is codified and readily accessible, the risk of not knowing what to do if something goes wrong is much lower*" (Massingham, 2018, p. 743).
2. Complexity. Determined by the amount of new knowledge that must be created to manage the risk factor, it is called the degree of creativity (DoC). DoC is measured by knowledge levels. If the knowledge necessary to manage the risk is extremely complex, the organization becomes vulnerable because affected by loss or unavailability, this knowledge must be recreated. Alternatively, if the required knowledge required is simple, it is likely to be easier to replace. "*Deeper levels of knowledge require more time to learn and, therefore, increase the possibility of inaction, i.e. when no one knows what to do*" (Massingham, 2018, p. 743).

2.4.4.3 Organizational Characteristics

1. Potential capacity. Potential capacity. Determined by the knowledge base of the organization, and defined as Risk Management Capability (RMC). RMC is measured by the percentage of staff with the knowledge necessary to manage the risk factor (i.e., the unwanted event). *"If only one or a relatively few staff have sufficient knowledge, the organization has low RMC. It is vulnerable if these staff leave the organization or are unavailable for any reason"* (Massingham, 2018, p. 743).
2. Realized capacity. Determined by the organization's willingness to allocate staff resources, is defined as risk management motivation (RMM) is measured by the degree to which the organization replaces staff required to manage the risk factor. Knowledge is about action and it must be put to some use in order to create value. *"The organization might have many staff who know what to do to manage the risk factor (i.e. high RMC) but not release them to perform this role, or the staff themselves may be unwilling to take on this role"* (Massingham, 2018, p. 743).

The combination of the knowledge risk characteristics with the six constructs shows the knowledge risk score. This measure is used to quantify the impact of knowledge loss necessary to manage risky events. In combination with the traditional decision tree method of probability and consequences, i.e., the risk score, it generates a general knowledge risk score. The result is a measure of the loss of knowledge that is different in that it focuses on work rather than on the individual. Hence, it is a measure of the knowledge loss about the job itself.

2.4.4.4 Organizational Problems

Knowledge Management performance is measured through changes in important and recurring organizational problems. Seven questions arise in this regard (Table 2.1).

Changes in these organizational issues can provide a measure of the knowledge loss caused by staff turnover. Organizations are frequently faced with challenges like high proportions of new staff or low morale (Massingham, 2018, 2019a). It may happen that in case of worsening of these problems, Knowledge Management is not able to solve it satisfactorily. This should not suggest KM inefficiencies, but rather such a negative knowledge loss impact that KM alone is not enough to deal with

Table 2.1 KM performance measurement: problems and solutions

Problems	*Solutions*
New staff in large proportions, due to a high turnover of operators, or the advanced age of the workforce	Better organizational learning. In this way, the Knowledge Management performances shorten the time of competence of the new staff. It follows that the negative impact of knowledge loss is measured by a longer time required for organizational learning
Presence of large proportions of young staff due to the exit of older staff	Better sharing of experience. In doing so, Knowledge Management performance implements experience sharing of older staff with younger staff. The negative impact knowledge loss is measured by longer times to gain experience, i.e. into less creativity, innovation and problem solving
High proportions of incompetent staff caused by poor workforce planning	Objective decision models (strategic alignment). Knowledge Management performance ensures that the right people are in the right place. The negative impact of knowledge loss is measured by a greater percentage of incompetent personnel
High proportions of staff with weak social networks	Improve social network structure (connectivity). The negative impact of knowledge loss is measured by a worse connectivity
Poor corporate governance	Providing customers with better risk management. Knowledge Management performance increases confidence in work outputs. Therefore, negative impact of knowledge loss is measured by low customer satisfaction (worse risk management)
The lack of communications or relations with stakeholders affects the organization's ability to explain how it creates value	Improve stakeholder satisfaction with the organization's performance (value management). Knowledge Management performance improves stakeholders' perception of the value of the organization, therefore the negative impact of loss of knowledge is measured by the reduction of stakeholder satisfaction (worse value management)

(continued)

Table 2.1 (continued)

Problems	*Solutions*
Staff dissatisfaction with work (emotional relationship with your organization)	Improvement of human resource management. KM's performance reduces employee turnover and increases productivity and quality of work; therefore, the negative impact of loss of consciousness is measured by the reduction of job satisfaction and organizational commitment

Source Our elaboration from Massingham, P. and Massingham, R. (2014), Does Knowledge Management Produce Practical Outcomes, *Journal of Knowledge Management*, 18 (2): 221–254, and from Massingham, P. (2019a), *Knowledge Management Theory in Practice*, Sage Publications Ltd., London, UK

it. In cases like these, the meaning of knowledge loss and its measurement emerge. The latter focuses on KM and not on the individual, thus measuring the impact of knowledge loss on organizational performance (Massingham, 2019b).

2.5 Knowing Knowledge Risks: Types, Characteristics, and Their Potential Harmfulness

Despite significant contributions from scholars as Durst and Massingham et al., to date, there is still a substantial immaturity of the body of knowledge regarding KRM. In fact, in a more recent review, Durst (2019) highlighted that, although research on Knowledge Risk Management has been quantitatively and qualitatively increased, the need for a better organization of the topic is still strong. The need to move beyond the boundaries of organizational types is also highlighted, considering in research not only those which by nature or because they are recipients of specific regulations have a deep-rooted culture of risk, such as banks or other companies in the financial sector. Anyway, precisely with reference to this last type of organization, as will be seen below in the present book, it is surprising how scientific production on KRM is to date really scarce.

Deriving from inefficiencies in knowledge management, knowledge risks refer to the possibility that organizations may suffer losses due to incorrect identification, storage, and protection of knowledge (Perrot, 2006, 2007). Among definitions of knowledge risks provided by Durst and Zięba, the one referring to them as "the measure of the probability and severity of adverse effects of any activities engaging or related somehow to the knowledge that can affect the functioning of an organization on any level" (Durst & Zięba, 2018, p. 256), makes the idea of how these risks may disturb, in part or in whole, the process that goes from knowledge acquisition to its application in organization's operational practice (Durst & Zięba, 2017).

According to their origin, knowledge risks have been classified into human, technological, and operational, the first category including knowledge risks associated with human resources management, thus connected with social, cultural and psychological factors; new technologies bring with them not only opportunities for organizations, but also the possibility of being exposed to knowledge risks deriving from their use; finally, knowledge risks that originate from the daily operations of organizations, such as mergers, outsourcing, or applying wrong or obsolete knowledge in operations, are part of the operational category (Durst & Zięba, 2018). In addition to classifying knowledge risks basing on their origin, Durst and Zięba (2017) first proposed a taxonomy aimed at their precise identification, description, and analysis. Thanks to this taxonomy, the possible uncertainties, and inaccuracies in the study of knowledge risks are also reduced, starting from the correct naming, which is not always simple, clear, and defined.

Before Durst and Zięba, therefore, studies on knowledge risks dealt with this topic in a rather fragmented way, and far from a detailed description, classification and distinction of the different knowledge risks. These scholars have the merit of contributing to the development of a systematic and independent line of research on Knowledge Risk Management. Thanks to their contributions, we can refer to the following types of knowledge risks: *Risk of Knowledge Loss, Risk of Knowledge Waste, Risk of Knowledge Spillover, Risk of Knowledge Hoarding, Risk of Knowledge Hiding, Risk of Knowledge Unlearning, Risk of Knowledge Forgetfulness, Risk of Knowledge Outsourcing, and Risk of Knowledge Digitization* (Durst & Henschel, 2020; Durst & Zięba, 2017, 2018; Durst et al., 2018).

After this brief digression on knowledge risks in general, a sort of "Identity Card" for each of the well-known knowledge risks is below proposed, with the aim of providing a synthetic information framework of: (a) their origins, (b) main features, (c) their potential of harmfulness, (d) how they are considered by different organizations, (e) case studies harbingers of important information for their prevention and mitigation. We believe that these identification cards could be useful for having an immediate and quite complete reference of knowledge risks, and that in some way they could contribute also to development of KRM strand, even if just supportive in the first approaches to knowledge risks. According to this, and basing on findings of the studies mentioned above, in the following sections, "ID cards" of most well-known knowledge risks so far identified will be presented.

2.5.1 *Risk of Knowledge Loss*

2.5.1.1 *Definition, Origin, and Classifications*

The risk of knowledge loss (not to be confused with the knowledge activation risk) has a dual nature. It is both a human and technological knowledge risk. With reference to its human origin, risk of knowledge loss could manifest itself every time in an organization human resource management strategies are implemented. The risk of knowledge loss, therefore, could be really insidious because it could become unavoidable in response to phenomena as employee turnover—voluntary or involuntary – or to accidents as death or illness of employee (Durst & Zięba, 2017). In the event that knowledge loss originates from technological factors, it could manifest itself as a consequence of the loss of any personal contributions to technological supports (for example, an implementation of a customer database with information derived from direct customer relationship of retired employee).

According to Durst and Zięba (2017), the risk of knowledge loss cannot be classified neither among knowledge risks originating from within the organization, nor among those that originate from the outside, but it can be placed at the ideal intersection between organization and external environment; moreover, being connected with knowledge work, it is characterized by continuity and not accidentality and is inherent in the human component of the organization (employees). Risk of knowledge loss is also connected to multiple causality and can be connected to both tacit and explicit knowledge. To manage this knowledge risk, organizations could implement both preventive and law enforcement actions.

2.5.1.2 Potential Harmfulness

The risk of knowledge loss could have a significant impact on organizations of different types and sizes regardless of its origin. Over the years, as the field of Knowledge Risk Management was implemented, several scholars dealt with examining the possible consequences of knowledge loss. Most of the scientific production focused on the effects of workforce mobility on knowledge management of organizations. In this regard, Droege and Hoobler (2003) argued that employee turnover could cause loss of tacit knowledge, and stressed the positive correlation between tacit knowledge retention and the level of interaction, collaboration, and employee access to non-redundant information.

In other cases, impacts of departing employees are highlighted, considering the possibility that they take away with them precious type of specialized technical knowledge-related stored over the years (Sumbal, Tsui, Cheong, & See-to, 2018; Joe, Yoong, & Patel, 2013). The risk of knowledge loss could also occur in the context of project development due to developers' turnover; it may happen, in fact, that when one or more developers leave the project, their knowledge could be lost if remaining developers are unable to understand the design choices of those retired (Nassif & Robillard, 2017; Rashid, Clarke, & O'Connor, 2019). In other studies, the impact of the knowledge loss risk in its technological nature is analyzed, as in the case of serious production accidents caused precisely by the loss of important technological knowledge (Silva, 2017); while, in others, methodologies for its assessment and mitigation are proposed (Massingham, 2010, 2018, 2019a).

2.5.1.3 Risk of Knowledge Loss in Organizations

In a recent study, the risk of knowledge loss was found to be the most considered by organizations belonging to different sectors (Durst et al., 2018).

Like any other type of risk, the risk of knowledge loss cannot be eliminated, but only prevented and mitigated.

2.5.2 Risk of Knowledge Waste

2.5.2.1 Definition, Origin, and Classifications

Belonging to the category of operational knowledge risks, risk of knowledge waste could occur in situations where the knowledge in the possession of the organization—and potentially valuable—is not used;

it always originates within the organization (employees), and has the character of randomness. Furthermore, given its nature, organizations have the possibility of acting directly on risk of knowledge waste for its prevention or possible mitigation (Durst & Zięba, 2017). Ferenhof, arguing that the risk of knowledge waste basically comes from a failure of converting knowledge process, identified as its possible manifestations: (i) reinvention, (ii) lack of system discipline, (iii) underutilized people, (iv) scatter, (v) hand-off, and (vi) wishful thinking. Reinvention refers to knowledge waste related to the organization's failure to exploit solutions, components, projects, experiences or knowledge previously created and/or acquired; lack of system discipline, on the other hand, concerns the quality of the organizational objectives, in the sense of a lack of clarity about objectives, roles, rules, and responsibilities; underutilized people relates to the lack of use by staff of skills that they could instead use for a more effective process; scatter refers, however, to actions that make knowledge ineffective due to the interruption of interactions required for collaboration; hand-off occurs when knowledge, responsibility, action, and feedback are separated, causing decisions made by who do not have enough experience to make them effectively; and finally, wishful thinking, based on subjective reasoning rather than rational reasoning, corresponds to operating blindly, without consistent support data (Ferenhof, Durst, & Selig, 2015).

2.5.2.2 *Potential Harmfulness*

Potential harmfulness of knowledge waste depends both on the quantity of unused knowledge, and on the importance that this knowledge has for the operations within the organization (Durst & Zięba, 2018). The main literature on risk of knowledge waste and its impact on organizations has been revised in a paper which clearly shows that the body of knowledge regarding this topic is still underdeveloped (Ferenhof et al., 2015). This research shows that most of the contributions are focused on the importance of knowledge reuse against the implications of the knowledge waste risk.

2.5.2.3 *Risk of Knowledge Waste in Organizations*

With reference to the incidence of knowledge waste in organizations, in a list of the most common knowledge risks, it appears to be an average risk spread in organizations of different types and sizes (Durst et al., 2018).

Like any other type of risk, the risk of knowledge waste cannot be eliminated, but only prevented and mitigated.

2.5.3 *Risk of Knowledge Spillover*

2.5.3.1 Definition, Origin, and Classifications

Organizations could be exposed to the risk of knowledge spillover if valuable knowledge leaves the organization and ends up to competitors that use it to their advantage. By occurring randomly, the risk of knowledge spillover originates from outside the organization (co-operants, competitors) and relates to the relationships that the latter maintains with the external environment (Durst & Zięba, 2017).

2.5.3.2 Potential Harmfulness

In general, the impact of knowledge risks may be negative or positive (Durst & Zięba, 2017). Some types of knowledge risks could have both negative and positive impacts on organizations; this is precisely the case of knowledge spillover, because the organization whose valuable knowledge has been spilled out suffers the negative effect, while the competitor who acquired this knowledge benefits from the relative positive impact; this is the case, for example, of the positive relationship between knowledge spillovers and R&D investment, in the sense that, thanks to its own R&D, organizations can exploit the knowledge of competitors (Aghion & Jaravel, 2015; Cohen, & Levinthal, 1989; Ding & Huang, 2010).

2.5.3.3 Risk of Knowledge Spillover in Organizations

As the risk of knowledge loss, knowledge spillover is among the most common knowledge risk in organizations of different sectors and sizes (Durst et al., 2018).

Like any other type of risk, the risk of knowledge spillover cannot be eliminated, but only prevented and mitigated.

2.5.4 *Risk of Knowledge Hoarding*

2.5.4.1 Definition, Origin, and Classifications

Considered together with knowledge hiding as one of the two constructs of not-sharing information, the risk of knowledge hoarding is defined as "the act of accumulating knowledge which may or may not be shared in the future; that is, it is knowledge that has not been requested by another individual" (Webster et al., 2008, p. 6), "an individual's deliberate and strategic concealment of information, and perceived hoarding, defined as coworkers' beliefs that an individual is engaged in hoarding" (Evans, Hendron, & Oldroyd, 2015, p. 494). From these definitions, it is clear how risk of knowledge hoarding originates within the organization (employees), and belongs to human knowledge risks category (Durst & Zięba, 2018).

2.5.4.2 Potential Harmfulness

Given that knowledge hoarding does not necessarily imply an intentionality of the employee to accumulate information and keep it secret in order to damage the organization—perhaps it is information that causes distress in case of sharing—(Webster et al., 2008), however, its potential harmfulness remains a possible danger to organizations. In the literature, there seem to be conflicting opinions on the theme of knowledge hoarding, considered, in fact, both a topic that is still recent and not widely addressed (Durst & Zięba, 2018), and a research field with a past of more than twenty years of scientific production (Trusson, Hislop, & Doherty, 2017). Despite this, a relationship of reciprocity has been identified between knowledge hoarding and negative response acts, in the sense that non-knowledge sharing behaviors could be perceived as selfish and opportunistic, and could be reciprocated by social sanctions in the form of negative acts (Holten, Hancock, Persson, Hansen, & Høgh, 2016). Furthermore, the risk of knowledge hoarding, by reducing knowledge sharing, could influence organizational culture. In fact, employees who have accumulated knowledge in conjunction with a request for help, are pushed to continue this accumulation, thus starting a vicious circle, with disadvantage for the whole organization (Durst & Zięba, 2018).

2.5.5 Risk of Knowledge Hoarding in Organizations

In the study by Durst et al. (2018) that investigates the types of knowledge risks included in the organizations' risk management, risk of knowledge hoarding is among the least considered by organizations.

Like any other type of risk, the risk of knowledge hoarding cannot be eliminated, but only prevented and mitigated.

2.5.6 *Risk of Knowledge Hiding*

2.5.6.1 Definition, Origin, and Classifications

As anticipated dealing with knowledge hoarding, the risk of knowledge hiding is considered a construct of not-sharing information. It originates within the organization, and belongs to the category of human knowledge (Durst & Zięba, 2017). Connelly, Zweig, Webster, and Trougakos (2012, p. 65), defined the risk of knowledge hiding as "an intentional attempt by an individual to withhold or conceal knowledge that has been requested by another person," and provide an example of voluntary knowledge hiding, and one in which there is no will to act against the organization:

- Example 1. An employee asks the colleague for a copy of a document, the colleague provides him with a part, but not the entire document requested. In this case the knowledge hiding could be moved by deception.
- Example 2. An employee asks the college for a copy of a document and receives a denial as a response because the document is confidential and cannot be shared. In this case, knowledge hiding occurs but without deception.

From these examples, emerge as knowledge hiding, as long as correlated, remains distinct from some possible behaviors as: knowledge hoarding, knowledge sharing, counterproductive workplace behaviors (CWB), workplace aggression, social undermining in the workplace, workplace incivility, and deception (Connelly et al., 2012).

2.5.6.2 Potential Harmfulness

Although over time scholars have mainly dealt with issues related to positive and constructive organizational behaviors such as knowledge sharing, the topic of knowledge hiding has nevertheless attracted the attention of many researchers, especially with reference to the debate on knowledge protection (Manhart & Thalmann, 2015). Among these, Serenko and Bontis (2016), for example, highlighted some possible consequences of intra-organizational knowledge hiding, which substantially confirm its harmful potential. First of all, knowledge hiding could expose the organization to the duplication of that knowledge which, despite the possession of an employee, is not available due to a deliberate decision to not share it.

In addition, knowledge hiding behavior of some employees could negatively impact the organizational commitment of work colleagues; and furthermore, this counterproductive behavior could affect not only the quality of the organizational objectives, but can also have random effects on the organization's stakeholders.

2.5.6.3 *Risk of Knowledge Hiding* in Organizations

Referring also in this case to one of the few studies that provided an overview of the diffusion of knowledge risks in the various organizations (Durst et al., 2018), is possible to note a not wide consideration of knowledge hiding by organizations (it ranks among the last places after the knowledge waste and before knowledge hoarding).

Like any other type of risk, the risk of knowledge hiding cannot be eliminated, but only prevented and mitigated.

2.5.7 *Risk of Knowledge Unlearning*

2.5.7.1 *Definition, Origin, and Classifications*

Knowledge unlearning belongs to the category of human knowledge risks and for this reason it always originates within the organization (Durst & Zięba, 2017). Tsang and Zahra (2008) summarized some of the definitions of unlearning knowledge provided over the years by researchers. Among these, that of Akgun et al. according to which knowledge unlearning is the "process of reducing or eliminating pre-existing knowledge or habits"; or the one that defines knowledge unlearning as "forgetting the old and developing a better, more appropriate routine as a way of adapting to changed circumstances"; or again the definition proposed by Harvey and Buckley according to which knowledge unlearning refers to "systematic removal of information that is outdated or no longer useful to management decision-making."

2.5.7.2 *Potential Harmfulness*

The potential harmfulness of knowledge unlearning depends on the presence or absence of intentionality. In the sense that knowledge unlearning could have a negative impact on the organization when, to the deliberate unlearning process, an accidental loss of knowledge is combined, that is, devoid of any logic and awareness (Durst & Zięba, 2018).

2.5.7.3 *Risk of Knowledge Unlearning in Organizations*

This knowledge risk is more widespread than knowledge waste, hoarding, and hiding risks, and is in general fairly treated by organizations of different types and sizes (Durst et al., 2018).

Like any other type of risk, the risk of knowledge unlearning cannot be eliminated, but only prevented and mitigated.

2.5.8 *Risk of Knowledge Forgetfulness*

2.5.8.1 *Definition, Origin, and Classifications*

How organizations can create, share, hide, and unlearn knowledge, can also forget it. Risk of knowledge forgetfulness is a risk that originates within the organization and belongs to the category of human knowledge risks (Durst & Zięba, 2017). If we consider the importance of forgetting old knowledge to acquire new knowledge, knowledge forgetfulness can be considered as the abandonment of practices or entire strategies that were dominant, but which now hinder the acquisition of new knowledge and therefore also organization competitiveness. Holan and Phillips (2004) highlighted how knowledge forgetfulness is a complex phenomenon; in fact, it can be accidental or intentional, harmful or beneficial but, in any case, capable of impacting the competitiveness of the organization.

2.5.8.2 *Potential Harmfulness*

Due to its multiple nature, and its potentially negative effects, manage risk of knowledge forgetfulness becomes crucial for organizations. In fact, both in the case of accidental unlearning and in the intentional unlearning case, organizations must pay attention to the possible consequences of such situations; on the one hand, accidental unlearning could impact in terms of costs to recover knowledge already present but lost; on the other, knowledge unlearning is necessary for those organizations that have to forget old knowledge that blocks them in the past or keeps bad habits imported from other organizations (Holan & Phillips, 2004).

2.5.8.3 *Risk of Knowledge Forgetfulness in Organizations*

From the aforementioned study on knowledge risks in organizations (Durst et al., 2018) emerges how the risk of knowledge unlearning is considered in the risk management of organizations more or less like knowledge forgetting, standing at about half of the ranking reported in this study.

Like any other type of risk, the risk of knowledge forgetfulness cannot be eliminated, but only prevented and mitigated.

2.5.9 *Risk of Knowledge Outsourcing*

2.5.9.1 *Definition, Origin, and Classifications*

According to Durst and Zięba (2017, 2018) risk of knowledge outsourcing belongs to the category of operational knowledge risks, originates from the outside of the organization (co-operants), and is a risk attributable to a single potential cause (situation-specific risk).

2.5.9.2 *Potential Harmfulness*

Even outsourcing activities may involve organization's exposure to a series of knowledge risks. Examples are the possibility that skills and capabilities for managing central knowledge processes are lost by outsourcing business activities or functions; or the case of excessive identification with the client organization which may hinder the outsourcing activity, and consequently threaten the knowledge management of the organization of origin; or again, the possibility that contractors are underestimated by the most dangerous knowledge risks, instead giving more emphasis to the less harmful ones (Durst & Zięba, 2018).

2.5.9.3 *Risk of Knowledge Outsourcing in Organizations*

Together with knowledge loss and spillover risks, risk of knowledge outsourcing is widely considered by organizations from different sectors (Durst et al., 2018).

Like any other type of risk, the risk of knowledge outsourcing cannot be eliminated, but only prevented and mitigated.

2.5.10 *Risk of Knowledge Digitization*

2.5.10.1 *Definition, Origin, and Classifications*

Risk of knowledge digitization belongs to the category of technological knowledge risks. It originates within the organization and is connected to the use of digital technologies for the performance of corporate functions, including also knowledge management (Durst & Zięba, 2017).

2.5.10.2 *Potential Harmfulness*

Its potential harmfulness refers to the possibility that using digital technologies could expose organization to situations as the manipulation of algorithms used, with the effect of deterioration of information quality; or as the possibility that the use of technologies within the organization leads to neglecting the human element (Durst & Zięba, 2018).

2.5.10.3 *Risk of Knowledge Digitization in Organizations*

Although it can be said that organizations today operate in what has been called the "digital era," knowledge digitization risk stands at the end of the ranking of the diffusion of knowledge risks in organizations (Durst et al., 2018).

Like any other type of risk, the risk of knowledge digitization cannot be eliminated, but only prevented and mitigated.

References

Aghion, P., & Jaravel, X. (2015). Knowledge spillovers, innovation and growth. *The Economic Journal, 125*(583), 533–573.

Akhavan, P., Shahabipour, A., & Hosnavi, R. (2018). A model for assessment of uncertainty in tacit knowledge acquisition. *Journal of Knowledge Management, 22*(2), 413–431.

Borzillo, S., & Kaminska-Labbe, R. (2011). Unravelling the dynamics of knowledge creation in communities of practice though complexity theory lenses. *Knowledge Management Research & Practice, 9*, 353–366.

Bratianu, C. (2018). A holistic approach to knowledge risk. *Management Dynamics in the Knowledge Economy, 6*(4), 593–607.

Closs, D. J., Jacobs, M. A., Swink, M., & Webb, G. S. (2008). Toward a theory of competencies for the management of product complexity: Six case studies. *Journal of Operations Management, 26*(5), 590–610.

Cohen, W. M., & Levinthal, D. A. (1989). Innovation and learning: The two faces of R&D. *The Economic Journal, 99*(397), 569–596.

Connelly, C. E., Zweig, D., Webster, J., & Trougakos, J. P. (2012). Knowledge hiding in organizations. *Journal of Organizational Behavior, 33*(1), 64–88.

Corvellec, H. (2009). The practice of risk management: Silence is not absence. *Risk Management, 11*(3–4), 285–304.

Davis, B., & Sumara, D. (2006). *Complexity and education: Inquiries into learning, teaching and research*. Mahwah, NJ: Lawrence Erlbaum Associates.

DeLong, D. W. (2004). *Lost knowledge: Confronting the threat of an ageing workforce*. Oxford: Oxford University Press.

Ding, X., & Huang, R. (2010). Effects of knowledge spillover on inter-organizational resource sharing decision in collaborative knowledge creation. *European Journal of Operational Research, 201*(3), 949–959.

Droege, S. B., & Hoobler, J. M. (2003). Employee turnover and tacit knowledge diffusion: A network perspective. *Journal of Managerial Issues, 15*(1), 50–64.

Drucker, P. F. (1988). The coming of the new organization (Chapter 1). In *Harvard business review on knowledge management* (pp. 1–19). Boston, MA: Harvard Business School Press.

Durst, S. (2019). How far have we come with the study of knowledge risks? *VINE Journal of Information and Knowledge Management Systems, 49*(1), 21–34.

Durst, S., Bruns, G., & Henschel, T. (2018). The management of knowledge risks: What do we really know? In *Global business expansion: Concepts, methodologies, tools, and applications* (pp. 258–269). Hershey: IGI Global.

Durst, S., & Ferenhof, H. A. (2016). Knowledge risk management in turbulent times. In *Competitive strategies for small and medium enterprises* (pp. 195–209). Cham: Springer.

Durst, S., & Henschel, T. (2020). *Knowledge risk management: from theory to praxis*. Berlin: Springer.

Durst, S., Hinteregger, C., & Zięba, M. (2019). The linkage between knowledge risk management and organizational performance. *Journal of Business Research, 105,* 1–10.

Durst, S., & Zięba, M. (2017). Knowledge risks-towards a taxonomy. *International Journal of Business Environment, 9*(1), 51–63.

Durst, S., & Zięba, M. (2018). Mapping knowledge risks: Towards a better understanding of knowledge management. *Knowledge Management Research & Practice, 17*(1), 1–13.

Durst, S., & Zięba, M. (2020). Knowledge risks inherent in business sustainability. *Journal of Cleaner Production, 251,* 119670.

Durst, S., Zięba, M., & Aisenberg Ferenhof, H. (2018). Knowledge risk management in organizations. In *IFKAD 2018–13th International Forum on Knowledge Asset Dynamics,* 4–6 July, Delft.

Evans, J. M., Hendron, M. G., & Oldroyd, J. B. (2015). Withholding the ace: The individual-and unit-level performance effects of self-reported and perceived knowledge hoarding. *Organization Science, 26*(2), 494–510.

Ferenhof, H., Durst, S., & Selig, P. (2015). Knowledge waste in organizations: A review of previous studies. *Brazilian Journal of Operations & Production Management, 12*(1), 160–178.

Fisser, S., & Browaeys, M.-J. (2010). Team learning on the edge of chaos. *The Learning Organization, 17*(1), 58–68.

Grant, R. M. (1996). Toward a knowledge-based theory of the firm. *Strategic Management Journal, 17*(S2), 109–122.

Grant, R. (1997). The knowledge-based view of the firm: Implications for management practice. *Long Range Planning, 30*(3), 450–454.

Grant, R. (2002). The knowledge-based view of the firm (Chapter 8). In C. W. Choo & N. Bontis(Eds.), *The strategic management of intellectual capital and organizational knowledge*. New York: Oxford University Press.

Han, K. H., & Park, J. W. (2009). Process-centred knowledge model and enterprise ontology for the development of knowledge management system. *Expert Systems with Applications, 36,* 7441–7447.

Holan, P. M. D., & Phillips, N. (2004). Remembrance of things past? The dynamics of organizational forgetting. *Management Science, 50*(11), 1603–1613.

Holland, J. (2019). Bank top management teams, disclosure, learning, survival and failure—1990–2017. *Qualitative Research in Financial Markets, 11*(1), 31–59.

Holten, A. L., Hancock, G. R., Persson, R., Hansen, Å. M., & Høgh, A. (2016). Knowledge hoarding: Antecedent or consequent of negative acts? The mediating role of trust and justice. *Journal of Knowledge Management, 20*(2), 215–229.

Ilina, T., & Vargab, L. (2015). The uncertainty of systemic risk. *Risk Management, 17,* 240–275.

Jennex, M. E., & Durcikova, A. (2013). *Assessing knowledge loss risk*. Proceedings of 46th Hawaii International Conference on System Sciences (HICSS), 7–10 January, Wailea, HI, pp. 3478–3487.

Joe, C., Yoong, P., & Patel, K. (2013). Knowledge loss when older experts leave knowledge-intensive organisations. *Journal of Knowledge Management, 17*(6), 913–927.

Kallenberg, K. (2009). Operational risk management in Swedish industry: Emergence of a new risk paradigm? *Risk Management, 11*(2), 90–110.

Lee, S., Suh, E., & Lee, M. (2014). Measuring the risk of knowledge drain in communities of practice. *Journal of Knowledge Management, 18*(2), 382–395.

Manhart, M., & Thalmann, S. (2015). Protecting organizational knowledge: A structured literature review. *Journal of Knowledge Management, 19*(2), 190–211.

Massingham, P. (2010). Knowledge risk management: A framework. *Journal of Knowledge Management, 14*(3), 464–485.

Massingham, P. (2018). Measuring the impact of knowledge loss: An empirical longitudinal study. *Journal of Knowledge Management, 22*(4), 721–758.

Massingham, P. (2019a). *Knowledge management theory in practice*. London, UK: Sage.

Massingham, P. (2019b). Second track processes: A research agenda. *Journal of Behavioural Economics and Social Systems, 1*(1), 29–50.

Massingham, P. (2019c), *An Aristotelian interpretation of practical wisdom the case of retirees.* Palgrave Communications, pp. 1–13.

Massingham, P. (2019d, forthcoming). Emergent communities of practice: A complexity theory lens. *Journal of Behavioural Economics and Social Systems, 2*(1).

Massingham, P., & Massingham, R. (2014). Does knowledge management produce practical outcomes. *Journal of Knowledge Management, 18*(2), 221–254.

Nassif, M., & Robillard, M. P. (2017, September). Revisiting turnover-induced knowledge loss in software projects. *In 2017 IEEE International Conference on Software Maintenance and Evolution* (ICSME) (pp. 261–272). IEEE.

Nonaka, I., & Takeuchi, H. (1995). *The knowledge-creating company: How Japanese companies create the dynamics of innovation.* Oxford: Oxford University Press.

Perrott, B. E. (2006). Knowledge management in health: An evolution. *Proceedings of Knowledge Management: The Key to Innovative Health Programs.*

Perrott, B. E. (2007). A strategic risk approach to knowledge management. *Business Horizons, 50*(6), 523–533.

Polanyi, M., & Prosch, H. (1975). *Meaning.* Chicago: University of Chicago Press.

Rashid, M., Clarke, P. M., & O'Connor, R. V. (2019). A systematic examination of knowledge loss in open source software projects. *International Journal of Information Management, 46,* 104–123.

Rothenburger, B., & Galarreta, D. (2006). Facing knowledge evolution in space project: A multi-viewpoint approach. *Journal of Knowledge Management, 10*(2), 52–65.

Serenko, A., & Bontis, N. (2016). Understanding counterproductive knowledge behavior: Antecedents and consequences of intra-organizational knowledge hiding. *Journal of Knowledge Management, 20*(6), 1199–1224.

Silva, E. C. (2017). Accidents and the technology. *Journal of Loss Prevention in the Process Industries, 49,* 319–325.

Smith, E. A. (2001). The role of tacit and explicit knowledge in the workplace. *Journal of knowledge Management, 5*(4), 311–321.

Stam, D. C. (2009). Intellectual liabilities: lessons from The Decline and Fall of the Roman Empire. *VINE, 39*(1), 92–104.

Sumbal, M., Tsui, E., Cheong, R., & See-to, E. (2018). Critical areas of knowledge loss when employees leave in the oil and gas industry. *Journal of Knowledge Management, 22*(7), 1573–1590.

Trusson, C., Hislop, D., & Doherty, N. (2017). The rhetoric of "knowledge hoarding": A research-based critique. *Journal of Knowledge Management, 21*(6), 1540–1558.

Tsang, E., & Zahra, S. (2008). Organizational unlearning. *Human relations, 61*(10), 1435–1462.

Tsoukas, H. (2005). Do we really understand tacit knowledge. *Managing Knowledge: An Essential Reader, 107,* 1–18.

Wah, L. (2000). Making knowledge stick. In *The knowledge management yearbook, 2001* (pp. 145–156).

Waldrop, M. (1992). *Complexity: The emerging science at the edge of order and chaos* (p. 12). New York, NY: Simon & Schuster.

Webster, J., Brown, G., Zweig, D., Connelly, C. E., Brodt, S., & Sitkin, S. (2008). Beyond knowledge sharing: Withholding knowledge at work. *Research in Personnel and Human Resources Management, 27*(8), 1–37.

Zagzebski, L. (2017). What is knowledge? In *The Blackwell guide to epistemology* (pp. 92–116).

Zhang, J., Jiang, H., Wu, R., & Li, J. (2018). Reconciling the dilemma of knowledge sharing: A network pluralism framework of firms' R&D alliance network and innovation performance. *Journal of Management, 20*(10), 1–31.

CHAPTER 3

Knowledge Management, Risk Management, Knowledge Risk Management: What Is Missing (or Messed) in Financial and Banking Sectors

Abstract The purpose of this chapter is to investigate the state of research on Knowledge Risk Management in banks and other financial firms. In particular, the chapter is aimed at verifying the shortage of research contributions on Knowledge Risk Management with specific reference to organizations belonging to banking and financial sectors. First, recent trends in knowledge management in banks and other financial firms has been pointed. Second, strengths and weaknesses of today's risk management of these organizations has been considered as well. Then, a systematic review has been performed to verify the level of development of KRM research in the banking and financial sectors; to the best of the author's knowledge, to date, a systematic review with this specific objective has not yet been conducted. Findings highlighted a substantial lack of contributions in this strand, as a clear reference to knowledge risks could not be found in most of the reviewed studies.

Keywords Knowledge Management · Risk Management · Knowledge Risk Management · Banks · Financial firms · Systematic review

M. La Torre, *Risk in Banking*,
https://doi.org/10.1007/978-3-030-54498-0_3

3.1 Introduction

The plethora of contributions provided over the years on Knowledge Management confirms the crucial importance of this topic for organizations of different types and sizes. As highlighted previously in this book, research on Knowledge Management (KM) has progressively developed also through those studies focused on its linkage with Risk Management (RM), thus bringing out a further strand, Knowledge Risk Management (KRM), defined as "a systematic process of applying tools and techniques to identify, analyze and respond to risks associated with the creation, application and retention of organizational knowledge" (Durst, Bruns, & Henschel, 2016, p. 259). In this way, risk managers can implement organization's risk management by including risks associated with the use of knowledge, contributing even more to the protection of organizational competitiveness. Therefore, scholars'support becomes very important to improve organizational risk management, also including knowledge risks (Durst & Henschel, 2020).

Both KM and RM have a long tradition of scientific production. The same cannot be said for KRM strand, which is still considered in its infancy (Durst & Henschel, 2020). Over the past twenty years, in fact, the KM strand has reached such a maturity that its practices have been positively correlated with the organizational performance (Massingham & Massingham, 2014; Schiuma, 2012; Zack, McKeen, & Singh, 2009; et al.). Even Risk Management, although counting more research focused on organizations such as banks and insurance companies, that historically invest in risk management, is a consolidated and structured research field, both with reference to the analysis of its tools and techniques applied in different organizations (Alavi, 2017; Khodadadyan, Mythen, Assa, & Bishop, 2018; Ostrom & Wilhelmsen, 2019; Pasha, Qaiser, & Pasha, 2018; Rostami, 2016; et al.), both regarding its relationship with organizational performance (Callahan & Soileau, 2017; Gordon, Loeb, & Tseng, 2009; Kokobe & Gemechu, 2016; Shad, Lai, Fatt, Klemeš, & Bokhari, 2019; Soltanizadeh, Rasid, Golshan, & Ismail, 2016; et al.).

With reference to Knowledge Risk Management, instead, there is still work to be done to achieve a systematic and independent line of research, although there are already several contributions that also consider the risky side of knowledge (Bratianu, 2018; Durst & Zięba, 2017, 2018), and although some scholars have also recently dealt with the relationship between KRM and organizational performance (Durst, Hinteregger, & Zięba, 2019).

This situation seems to be even more evident with reference to the financial and banking sectors. In fact, there are not many contributions focused on knowledge risk management of organizations belonging to these sectors, such as banks, insurance companies, and other financial intermediaries.

Based on the above-described scenario, this chapter is aimed at verifying this shortage of research contributions, performing a systematic review. In order to contextualize this review, recent trends in knowledge management in banks and other financial firms are also pointed, and some aspects of strengths and weaknesses of today's risk management of these organizations are considered as well.

For this purpose, the chapter is organized as follows. Section 3.2, focuses on Knowledge Management in financial and banking sectors, highlighting some recent research trends. In Sect. 3.3, Risk Management challenges in the post-crisis banking system are considered; while the readiness of banks in Knowledge Risk Management is verified, in Sect. 3.4, through a systematic review aiming to identify those studies focused specifically on the experience of these organizations with knowledge risks.

3.2 Knowledge Management in Financial and Banking Sectors: Latest Research Trends

That knowledge is a crucial resources for organizations of all types and sizes, to date, is a common ground. Therefore, Knowledge Management can be considered one of the most relevant practices to achieve better organizational performance and long-term competitive advantage. This also applies to organizations belonging to the financial and banking sectors.

The global financial crisis has posed numerous challenges for banks. First, a reorganization of business models was required, with a return to "narrow banking" rather than commercial banking, that diversify into areas traditionally offered by investment banks and vice versa (Butzbach, 2014). Moreover, international harmonization of financial regulation becomes essential for stability protection of the entire financial system; the inadequacies of the Basel II Agreement can only be overcome thanks to progress in the capital regime regulation and in banking governance (Anagnostopoulos & Kabeega, 2018). Another of the main post-crisis challenges for banks was the need to adapt their operating methods to a greater number of regulatory requirements. In this sense, compliance of banking operations with the internal rules and standards imposed by supervisory authorities takes on a fundamental role for the correct implementation of post-crisis regulations in the banking sectors. This situation was exacerbated by greater competitive pressure for banks and other financial institutions also with reference to customers' knowledge in preparation for long-term loyalty (Chaikovska, 2019).

At the heart of all these developments, correct knowledge management becomes even more important and essential, thinking of it not only as a mere mechanism, but as a practice that can make a difference. Much seems to have changed since the results of the International Data Corporation (IDC) survey (2000), which highlighted that only 20% of Western European banks were engaged in knowledge management applications; or even compared to the findings in Cross and Weller (2001), involving around 300 banks and insurance companies, that found a substantial delay in the development of knowledge management approaches (Jayasundara, 2008). Much seems to have changed in the perception of the importance of knowledge management by scholars in the financial and banking sectors.

From a research point of view, attention to knowledge management tools and techniques applied in organizations of financial and banking sectors was intensified in the post-crisis period (Campanella, Derhy, & Gangi, 2019). Considering, instead, scientific production prior to or immediately following the crisis, works as the one by Sorrentino (1999) on the role of KM in banks, applying the Michael Earl model for the representation of KM components, found a substantial imbalance between the hard ones as IT, infrastructures and databases, and soft ones like human resources or learning culture. In 2005, Hung and Chou proposed a Knowledge Management Maturity (KMM) model, providing maturity paths that organizations can follow; the authors applied this model in three banks in Thailand to evaluate efforts in knowledge management practices (Hung & Chou, 2005). The relationship between intellectual capital and bank value creation was studied, in this period, by several scholars. Among them, Do Rosário Cabrita and Vaz (2005), which confirm the findings of previous works in the literature according to which intellectual capital is positively and significantly associated with organizational performance. In 2008, Curado also dealt with the topic of intellectual capital in the banking industry, addressing this subject with knowledge management such related concepts. Interviewing HR managers of 11 banking groups operating in Portugal, the author found that the most appreciated intellectual capital component is human capital, associated with the amount of tacit knowledge, that could be lost when individuals leave the organization (Curado, 2008).

In Yamagata (2002), a comparative analysis of Knowledge Management approach by American and Japanese banks was presented, highlighting that, despite different historical backgrounds of the two countries, KM can be successfully applied if elements are valued key as the use of both internal and external knowledge, or as organizational culture or human resources.

A case study on Central Bank of Malaysia is proposed by Ali and Ahmad (2006). In this work authors presented the components of the Banking Knowledge Management Model (BKMM), i.e., knowledge creation, conservation and sharing, and explained how each of these elements could be integrated to improve the quality of banking operations. In particular, they analyzed two case, one from Tiger Bank and the other from Camel Bank, to verify the progress of the knowledge management application.

Another empirical study was provided by Kridan and Goulding (2006), in which the benefits of applying and implementing a knowledge management system were seen in the improved performance of the banking sector in Libya. Other authors, instead, provided data on the implementation of KM practices in the banking sector in the Emirate of Abu Dabi (Alrawi & Elkhatib, 2009). Compared to the pre-crisis period, scientific production post-financial crisis seemed to be quantitatively and qualitatively more interested in KM issues in the financial and banking sectors. Some of the main trends of this period are summarized below.

For example, attention was paid to the opportunities offered by Customer Knowledge Management, both as a means of retaining customers, and as a driving force for the implementation of the innovation capability of bank management (MKM); and also to the benefits of Marketing Knowledge Management (MKM), in terms of achieving Sustainable Competitive Advantage (SCA) (Moosakhani, Haghighi, & Torkzadeh, 2012; Rezaee & Jafari, 2015; Taherparvar, 2014).

Other scholars dealt with the relationship between knowledge management and risk culture in banks, highlighting the awareness that the lack of the latter was considered one of the main causes of the global financial crisis (Geretto & Pauluzzo, 2015). Knowledge management practices in financial companies of developing countries continued to be addressed, to testify that knowledge management is recognized as an effective tool to be competitive in a difficult environment such as the post-crisis one (Li, 2013; Rashed, 2016). The determinants of the success of the Knowledge Management System in the banking industry were also considered, highlighting the importance of both technical and social factors, and also of user satisfaction (Cham, Lim, Cheng, & Lee, 2016; Irjayanti & Azis, 2013; Nattapol, Peter, & Laddawan, 2010).

Among the most recent research trends: studies on knowledge management impact on the relationship between bank indicators and Local Socioeconomic Development (LSED) indicators; on the analysis of Knowledge management lifecycle; and on the link between the knowledge creation process and banking performance (Campanella et al. 2019; Nurdin & Yusuf, 2020; Pons, Lezama, Izquierdo, Herrera, & Silva, 2020).

3.3 Risk Management Challenges in the Post-crisis Banking System

"The concept of risk is as old as mankind" (cited in Vasvàri, 2015, p. 29). This statement makes the idea of how long people have had to deal with risk, whether it is considered as the measure of the probability and severity of adverse effects or as a combination of the probability of an event and its consequences; or as the uncertainty of the result of actions and events; or as an uncertain consequence of an event or activity with respect to something that humans appreciate (cited in Aven, 2010); or a way to articulate a series of future scenarios that may vary through the available data and the methods of the topic (cited in Smallman, 1999). Many definitions, different perspectives, but the only certainty that risk, of any nature, cannot be eliminated, but only prevented or at the most mitigated. It remains a continuous presence in human action.

Over time, all organizations of all types and sizes applied tools and techniques to manage possible risks to which they may be exposed in the exercise of their activities. In its basic formulation, risk management consists of some main phases: (1) risks identification; (2) risk quantification and evaluation; (3) risk management and control; (4) risk development reporting. Strategies for risk management are entrusted to the directors' board, which also takes care of appointing the appropriate staff to deal with the phases mentioned above (Durst, & Ferenhof, 2016).

In this regard, Mongiardino and Plath (2010) also argued that effective banks' risk management should consider, at least, (a) the presence of a dedicated risk committee; (b) the independence of the majority of the members of this committee; and (c) the participation of the Chief Risk Officer in the bank's executive committees. Over the years, the approach to risk management has evolved highlighting the demand for greater requirements and the tendency to be broader and more integrated. It is not surprising, as Durst and Ferenhof (2016, pp. 198–199) pointed out, that the importance of risk management strategy has also been underlined in quality standards such as the ISO 9001: 2015, which in its revised version, requires companies to establish end-to-end processes for risk management, also consistent, accurate and extensive. Furthermore, according to ISO 31000:2018, the purpose of risk management is now "[...] the creation and protection of value. It improves performance, encourages innovation and supports the achievement of objectives." Therefore, risk management is seen as an integral part of all organizational activities (Durst & Henschel, 2020, p. 6). Most organizations, regardless activity carried out, adopt a series of approaches to risk management, guided both by the regulation to which they are addressed, and by the will of the board to fulfill their fiduciary duties toward shareholders and other stakeholders.

Risk management methods and criteria are contained in the safety and training policies of the various organizations (Calder & Watkins, 2010). Considering, then, that risk management is a process that involves people first and foremost, the precise identification of the contribution expected from each person to the organizational risk management process is very important. In this sense, the ISO 27005 standard, in its Clause 7.4, recommends that the organization and responsibilities of the information security risk management process should be established and maintained, and that the creation of an organization capable of carrying out a risk assessment could be considered as one of the resources required by ISO/IEC 27001(Calder & Watkins, 2010). Additionally, always in Durst and Ferenhof (2016) is highlighted how risk management should also examine the impact of different types of risks on each other, not leading to the interruption of commercial activities, but on the contrary facilitating their management in a more manageable and proactive way (Durst & Ferenhof, 2016).

In organizations belonging to the financial and banking sectors, such as banks and insurance companies, risk has historically been an integral part of corporate life. As for banks, in particular, risk culture is central and essential for prudent and solid management, having an impact on "risk appetite and policies, on types of risk assessment/yield and on final decisions. The behavior of banks and their staff is a direct expression of the culture of risk" (Carretta, Fiordelisi, & Schwizer, 2017, p. 3).

Nowadays, banking has become a complex business, no longer characterized simply by savings collection and lending activities. Banks' operations involve together Asset Liability Management (ALM), liquidity management, and risk management (Srinivasan, 2019). The concept of risk is inherent in financial activity, since this normally implies the transfer over time and/or space of values (means of payment, financial instruments) for this reason, subject to changes. In their typical activities, financial intermediaries assume and manage risks; and the better organized and managed they are, the better they manage these risks, transforming their attitude into profit opportunities (Corigliano, 2004). Main risks banks have to deal with are:

- credit risk, represents the main risk to which the bank is subjected in the exercise of its typical activity, (granting of credit lines, acquisition of debt securities issued by companies). This risk emerges every time there is a debt relationship such as to entail a payment commitment in favor of the bank which, if not honored, can result in a loss;
- market risks, are those connected to any changes in market factors that can influence the value of the equity, bond, and loan portfolios of financial intermediaries. Interest rate risk, price risk, and exchange rate risk belong to the category of market risks. Interest risk is linked to the impact of changes in the structure due to the expiration of interest rates on the value of interest sensitive assets held by financial intermediaries; the price risk, on the other hand, relates to the characteristic of the share prices of dispersing their returns over time around a medium value; while the impact of changes in exchange rate levels on the value of foreign currency positions held by financial intermediaries, identifies the risk of exchange;
- liquidity risk, refers to bank's inability to finance asset increases, and fulfill obligations on maturity, without incurring unacceptable losses. Banks are particularly sensitive to this risk, given their role in transforming short-term deposit maturities into long-term loans. Virtually, every transaction or financial commitment has implications for the bank's liquidity (BCBS, 2008);

- operational risk, is a category of risk implicit in any business activity, substantially attributable to malfunctions in the organizational systems and processes. Therefore, these risks can derive from inefficiencies in internal processes, from incompetence or non-fulfillment of human resources, from malfunctions of the technological apparatus, and from external factors such as environmental catastrophes or criminal activities or socio-political changes. For these reasons, compared to other types of risks, the operational ones presents distinctive characteristics such as, not being connected to an expected return, being transversal to any banking activity, and also being of complex identification and prevention (Birindelli & Ferretti, 2017).

Considering these risks, and especially regarding banks' role in the financial and payment systems, it is clear how an efficient and effective risk management is fundamental to guarantee the profitability and solidity of the bank itself and, consequently, of all the economic system. In last decades, banking has been influenced by introduction of new and increasingly sophisticated technologies, which have contributed to changing various operational aspects, such as production and management of financial instruments and advanced trading activity. These changes, although brought about by progress, if on the one hand favored financial companies development, on the other, expose them to always different and insidious types of risks. The global financial crisis found these organizations, in particular the banks, substantially unprepared for the turbulence of the financial markets, and with a risk management not completely adequate to meet such demanding challenges. Hence, risk management in such organizations has become the primary concern of bank regulators and policymakers (Quang & Gan, 2019). In fact, starting from this scenario, the Basel Committee for Banking Supervision (BCBS) proceeded with a diagnostic activity in order to highlight the main sources of criticality, and established a consequent updating and improvement of regulatory standards, with the aim of preventing the repetition of these inefficiencies. In particular, the main objectives of this reform activity concerned: (i) strengthening of global capital and liquidity regulations, thus promoting the resilience of the banking sector; (ii) improvement of the ability of the banking sector to absorb the shocks deriving from financial stress, so as to also reduce the risk of systemic contagion (Laurens, 2012). To achieve these goals, and in attempt to strengthen the micro-prudential regulation associated with the previous Basel I and II Agreements, Basel III, while adding a macro-prudential overlap, proposed modification in the following areas (McNamara, Wedow, & Metrick, 2019): (1) *Capital reform*. Banks were asked for the qualitative and quantitative improvement of their capital. The minimum ratio between ordinary shares and risk-weighted assets (RWA) was increased from 2 to 4.5%, with the total capital required to represent at least 8% of RWA. In addition, Basel III established a leverage ratio that requires banks to maintain Tier 1 capital of at least 3% of total exposure. (2) *Liquidity standards*. Two new liquidity measurements were introduced. With reference to the liquidity coverage ratio, banks must maintain a sufficient quantity of high-quality liquid assets to cover the outflows expected in a 30-day stressed financing scenario. (3) *Systemic risk and interconnection*. Given the threat of risk contagion due to the interconnection existing in the financial markets, higher capital requirements were required for systemic derivatives and inter-financial exposures. In addition, BCBS established a Large Exposure Framework for limiting the exposure that an internationally active bank could have toward a single counterparty.

The Financial Stability Board (FSB) also developed principles aimed at strengthening the supervision of systemically important financial institutions, financial institutions and groups in general, including insurers, securities companies and other non-bank financial institutions. Key elements of these principles were: (i) an effective risk appetite framework; (ii) a declaration of effective Risk Appetite Framework; (iii) risk limits; (iv) the definition of the roles and responsibilities of the board of directors and senior management (FSB, 2013). With particular reference to the Risk Appetite Framework (RAF), FSB principles highlighted how it defines financial institutions' risk profile, and that is part of the process of determining the risks assumed in relation to the risk capacity of institutions. So, an effective RAF should: *"a) include key background information and assumptions that informed the financial institution's strategic and business plans at the time they were approved; b) be linked to the institution's short- and long-term strategic, capital and financial plans, as well as compensation programs; c) establish the amount of risk the financial institution is prepared to accept in pursuit of its strategic objectives and business plan; d) determine for each material risk and overall the maximum level of risk that the financial institution is willing to operate within, based on its overall risk appetite, risk capacity, and risk profile; e) include quantitative measures that can be translated into risk limits applicable to business lines and legal entities as relevant; f) include qualitative statements that articulate clearly the motivations for taking on or avoiding certain types of risk; g) ensure that the strategy and risk limits of each business line and legal entity, as relevant, align with the institution-wide risk appetite statement as appropriate; h) be forward looking"* (FSB, 2013, pp. 5–6). A well-developed and articulated RAF through the declaration on risk appetite should also be closely interconnected with the Internal Capital Assessment Process (ICAAP), i.e., the Internal Capital Adequacy Assessment Process defined in Article 73 of Directive 2013/36/EU (CRD IV—Capital Requirements Directive 4): *"Financial institutions have valid, effective and global strategies and processes to evaluate and maintain on an ongoing basis the amounts, the composition and the distribution of internal capital that they deem adequate to cover the nature and level of the risks to which they are or could be exposed."* The CRD IV and the related Regulation 2013/575/EU (CRR—Capital Requirements Regulation) define the organic regulatory and control framework for banks and investment firms by accepting the contents of the Third Basel Capital Agreement.

A recent guide published by the European Central Bank (BCE, 2018) highlighted, then, how the main objective of the ICAAP is to contribute to the continuity of the financial institution from a capital perspective, ensuring that it has sufficient capital to bear its risks, absorb losses and pursue a sustainable strategy, even during a prolonged period of unfavorable trends: the objective of the institution's continuity must be reflected in the RAF, and the ICAAP should be used to examine the risk appetite and tolerance thresholds within the context of its overall capital constraints, considering the risk profile and vulnerabilities. The conditions that guarantee solidity, effectiveness, and exhaustiveness to the ICAAP rest on two pillars: the economic perspective and the regulatory perspective. The two perspectives, which should be complementary and provide information to each other, are based, respectively, on (BCE, 2018, p. 23):

- *Internal regulatory perspective:* continuous compliance with all relevant regulatory requirements and external constraints; medium-term projections of at least three years; takes into account all relevant risks (not just first pillar risks); considers imminent changes to legal, regulatory and accounting structures; adequate and consistent internal methods for quantifying the effects on the first pillar coefficients; additional management reserves determined by the entity.

- *Internal economic perspective*: hedging with internal capital of the risks that can cause economic losses; capital adequacy concept based on economic value considerations; internal definition of capital; internal methods for quantifying adequate and consistent risks; internal indicators, thresholds, and management reserves.

Despite this commitment by institutions and authorities, briefly above summarized, to date, several critical issues still remain.

Koh (2019), for example, argued that some problems that still afflict banks even years after the crisis, largely depend on their difficulties in finding adequately qualified risk management professionals. In this regard, the author proposed a more deliberate, proactive, and sustainable longer-term solution to develop competences in risk management instead of a short-term reaction. "A widely accepted definition of competency, that refers to the appropriate knowledge, skills and attitude to perform a job well, and to the right traits of the head, hand and heart. Competency relates not only to abstract head knowledge. Knowledge without skills (i.e., taking appropriate action in an organizational setting) is not of much use" (Koh, 2019, p. 4).

Effective management is also crucial for the proper functioning of banks. In this regard, Dinesen (2020) found a substantial "absence" of management in banking. Not an absence in the strict sense, but as "banking" that dominating management; and when banks grow larger and more complex, this imbalance leads to a lack of management development as would happen to any other production company. Another recent study focused on risk management behavior in banking. In this work, authors identified the "desirable" risk management behavior by financial services staff, finding a significant negative association between individual risk tolerance and desirable risk management behavior (Sheedy & Lubojanski, 2018).

Therefore, Risk Management could always be open to improvement, especially in those organizations where the risk culture is deeply rooted. It is not surprising, in fact, that the application of machine learning techniques has recently been tested in the management of banking risk, offering the potential to transform the area of risk management, with the construction of more accurate risk-based models, supported by complex and nonlinear schemes within large data sets (Leo, Sharma, & Maddulety, 2019).

3.4 The Readiness of Banks in Knowledge Risk Management: A Systematic Review

Knowledge Risk Management (KRM) is considered a strand not yet fully developed, both in relation to the number of contributions, and with reference to its systematic organization. "The extant body of knowledge clearly shows that there is a strong need for more systematic research on risks related to knowledge and the risk management of these particular risks. And this research should be conducted in all types of organizations" (Durst & Henschel, 2020, p. 8). With regard to banks and others financial firms, from a research point of view, the gap in understanding seems even more marked, especially against the fields of Knowledge Management and Risk Management, which instead are much more developed and organized (see previous Sects. 3.2 and 3.3).

In this Section, a literature review dealing with KRM in financial and banking organizations is conducted, aiming to establish the state of the art of this specific research strand and, on this basis, to identify any gaps in current understanding. In order to collect empirical evidence that allows to satisfy the eligibility criteria at the basis of such review, an explicit and systematic method useful to minimize bias is chosen, thus providing more reliable results from which to draw conclusions and make decisions, i.e., the systematic review (Ward, Usher-Smith, & Griffin, 2019). Systematic review is "a review of a clearly formulated question that uses systematic and explicit methods to identify, select, and critically appraise relevant research, and to collect and analyze data from the studies that are included in the review" (Moher, Liberati, Tetzlaff, Altman, & Prisma Group, 2009, p. 874). The choice of the systematic review is made on the basis of its characteristics which differentiate it from traditional (or scoping) review. According to Jesson, Matheson, and Lacey (2011), in fact, traditional reviews and systematic reviews differ from each other on the basis of the following elements:

- **Objectives**. Traditional review aims to obtain a general framework for a broad understanding of the field; while the systematic review proposes a very specific purpose and objectives, for a narrower focus and a very specific review question;
- **Review process**. Predefined patterns are not provided in traditional review, allowing creativity and exploration; while systematic review is based on a transparent and documented process;

- **Studies' identification and selection**. With traditional review the research is intentionally done by the reviewer and consists in moving from one study to another, the systematic provides, instead, a rigorous and complete research of all studies, using predetermined criteria for studies' inclusion and exclusion;
- **Quality assessment, analysis, and summary of the included studies**. With traditional review, these operations are based on the auditor's opinion, and the summary of the selected studies is discursive; checklists to evaluate the methodological quality of the studies, short summary in tabular form are suitable for the systematic review;
- **Methodological report**. Traditional review does not necessarily include this; with the systematic, instead methodological report must be presented for transparency.

Several scholars delineated the procedure for performing systematic reviews. Jesson et al. (2011) identified the following key phases:

1. **Mapping the field**. It is the phase in which one wonders about what is known and if there are gaps in the knowledge of the field. The availability of relevant material is assessed and then the preparation of the revision plan is carried out, which includes: definition of the question or the research questions, identification of the keywords and the setting of the criteria for inclusion and exclusion of the studies.
2. **Comprehensive search**. In this phase, electronic databases are accessed by searching using keywords. These keywords are checked to test their effectiveness according to research questions; inclusion and exclusion criteria of the studies are also checked. Obtained results are then documented and summarized in numbered tables.
3. **Quality assessment**. Following the principle of the "research hierarchy," the studies are read in full by evaluating the quality and deciding whether to include or exclude them from the review. The reasons for the exclusion must be motivated by filling in a table in this regard.
4. **Data extraction**. Relevant data must be transcribed on a worksheet (pre-designed extraction sheet).
5. **Synthesis**. Data collected from the various studies must be summarized to understand what we already know and what we need to know more. It is possible, then, to proceed with a meta-analysis or a mathematical synthesis.

6. **Write-up**. Phase in which a balanced, impartial and complete report is written, using a systematic review format. The report creation process is presented to allow other researchers to replicate your review. It is necessary to disseminate to inform.

Petticrew and Roberts (2008), instead, proposed a procedure for carrying out systematic review based on twelve phases: (1) initial phase of defining research questions, also specifying other elements such as the sample, the time period of interest, and the cultural or other context in which the intervention is delivered; (2) phase of creation of a working group; (3) drafting of the revision protocol; (4) actual research of the studies to be included and excluded, with the extraction of relevant information from the selected studies; (5) screening of studies to list those that could be further reviewed; (6) further review of studies that could be included after viewing in full; (7) data extraction with a formal and systematic approach: from the studies that meet all the inclusion criteria, information regarding their findings, the applied methodologies, and the analyzed sample are extrapolated; (8) focus on the methodology used by studies that meet all inclusion criteria with the aim of identifying any important bias. This phase is supportive for the interpretation of the data and for summarizing the results of the primary studies; (9) summary of the studies included. The included studies must be integrated, taking into account: population variations, intervention (if any), context, study design, results, and the degree to which they are influenced by prejudgments. This integration can be carried out statistically (meta-analysis) and/or narrative; (10) Focus on effects of publication bias, and other internal and external biases; (11) report preparation phase which must include the details of the complete research, such as how many studies have been included, how many excluded in each phase and why. This information can be included for example in a flowchart; (12) final phase of the systematic review, which involves the dissemination of the results of the review.

Another useful contribution to the implementation of systematic reviews comes from Critical Appraisal Skills Programme (CASP, 2018), which outlined a check list that considers three broad issues the reviewer must bear in mind when carrying out a systematic review. The proposed checklist is in fact divided into three main sections, respectively, focused on: (A) the validity of the results of the review; (B) the results obtained from the review as a whole; (C) the contribution that the review could offer.

The present systematic review on KRM in organizations belonging to financial and banking sectors was conducted summarizing contributions mentioned above, and according to some scholars who applied this methodology in their studies. The review started with a research plan containing research questions to be answered, keywords for searching studies, and a set of inclusion and exclusion criteria (Table 3.1).

As anticipated, this systematic review follows a protocol as suggested by main reference literature (Cerchione & Esposito, 2016; Jesson et al., 2011; Ward et al., 2019), and therefore consists of the following phases:

- Search strategy
- Selection of studies
- Comprehensive search
- Quality assessment
- Data extraction
- Write-up results

Table 3.1 Research plan

Research questions	• What types of knowledge risks were covered in the studies? • What types of financial organizations were considered in the studies? • Which were the main findings of the studies?
Inclusion criteria	English language; peer-reviewed; Web of Science, Google Scholar, DeepDyve, JSTOR and Sage databases; Conference Proceedings; book; book chapters; publication date between 2001 and 2020
Exclusion criteria	Other languages than English; non-academic research; other databases than Web of Science, Google Scholar, DeepDyve, JSTOR and Sage databases; gray literature than Conference Proceedings; other publication date than 2001–2020 time span
Keywords	Knowledge risks, knowledge waste, knowledge loss, knowledge leakage, knowledge outsourcing, knowledge hiding, knowledge hoarding, knowledge forgetfulness, knowledge spillover, knowledge unlearning, knowledge digitization, bank, insurance companies, financial firm, financial sector, banking sector, finance, banking, financial institutions, Basel, Tier 1 capital, leasing, factoring

Source Our elaboration

Studies were selected using the databases Web of Science, Google Scholar, DeepDyve, JSTOR, and Sage, searching the ones published from 2001 to 2020, as Knowledge Risk management is a research topic which began to be distinguished with greater decision from Knowledge Management and Risk Management starting from the early 2000s. Search strategy was built by combining keywords with Boolean terms such as "AND," "OR" or "NOT," and also truncation useful for searching words with similar meanings but different endings (Ward et al., 2019). The query strings were: *"knowledge risk" AND ("bank" OR "banking" OR "financial firm" OR "financ*" OR "finance" OR "financial sector" OR "financial institution" OR "insurance" OR "Basel" OR "Tier" OR "leasing" OR "factoring"); "knowledge waste"AND ("bank" OR "banking" OR "financial firm" OR "financ*" OR "finance" OR "financial sector" OR "financial institution" OR "insurance" OR "Basel" OR "Tier" OR "leasing" OR "factoring"); "knowledge loss" AND ("bank" OR "banking" OR "financial firm" OR "financ*" OR "finance" OR "financial sector" OR "financial institution" OR "insurance" OR "Basel" OR "Tier" OR "leasing" OR "factoring"); "knowledge leakage" AND ("bank" OR "banking" OR "financial firm" OR "financ*" OR "finance" OR "financial sector" OR "financial institution" OR "insurance" OR "Basel" OR "Tier" OR "leasing" OR "factoring"); "knowledge outsourcing" AND ("bank" OR "banking" OR "financial firm" OR "financ*" OR "finance" OR "financial sector" OR "financial institution" OR "insurance" OR "Basel" OR "Tier" OR "leasing" OR "factoring"); "knowledge hiding" AND ("bank" OR "banking" OR "financial firm" OR "financ*" OR "finance" OR "financial sector" OR "financial institution" OR "insurance" OR "Basel" OR "Tier" OR "leasing" OR "factoring"); "knowledge hoarding" ("bank" OR "banking" OR "financial firm" OR "financ*" OR "finance" OR "financial sector" OR "financial institution" OR "insurance" OR "Basel" OR "Tier" OR "leasing" OR "factoring"); "knowledge forgetfulness" AND ("bank" OR "banking" OR "financial firm" OR "financ*" OR "finance" OR "financial sector" OR "financial institution" OR "insurance" OR "Basel" OR "Tier" OR "leasing" OR "factoring"); "knowledge spillover" AND ("bank" OR "banking" OR "financial firm" OR "financ*" OR "finance" OR "financial sector" OR "financial institution" OR "insurance" OR "Basel" OR "Tier" OR "leasing" OR "factoring"); "knowledge unlearning" AND ("bank" OR "banking" OR "financial firm" OR "financ*" OR "finance" OR "financial sector" OR "financial institution" OR "insurance" OR "Basel" OR "Tier" OR "leasing" OR "factoring");*

"knowledge digit risk" AND ("bank" OR "banking" OR "financial firm" OR "financ*" OR "finance" OR "financial sector" OR "financial institution" OR "insurance" OR "Basel" OR "Tier" OR "leasing" OR "factoring").*

This review included studies published from January 2001 to February 2020. The reading of the papers considered relevant after the scanning of the abstracts led to the formation of the final list of 12 studies, which satisfy the selection criteria, and which were analyzed. Then, according to Cerchione and Esposito (2016) and Edvardsson and Durst (2014), to evaluate the 12 selected studies, a general view analysis were provided, identifying the following perspectives (Table 3.2):

- Studies over times
- Studies across journals
- Studies by research aims/objectives
- Studies by methodology
- Studies by main findings

Of the 12 studies analyzed in this systematic review, the most recent publication dated back to 2001 (one study), while the most recent are from 2020 (three studies); a work from 2008, one from 2010, one from 2011, one from 2012, two from 2015, one from 2016 and one from 2018. Respect to the research methodologies applied in the analyzed studies, the most common was case study method with interviews (six studies used it). The studies included also revealed a discrete geographical dispersion of research on KRM in the banking and financial sectors. The countries concerned are the following: China, Germany, Japan, Iran, Italy, South Africa (three studies could not be assigned).

Based on their main findings, the studies analyzed were clustered with respect to the following topic areas, in order to obtain a full overview of the problem: (1) Knowledge risks as an obstacle to knowledge sharing within organizations belonging to banking and financial sectors; (2) Lack of skills for identifying knowledge risks; (3) Proposals of frameworks or methods for management of knowledge risks. With reference to the first thematic area, four analyzed studies were included. Abzari et al. (2011) and Huang and Davison (2008) identified the loss of knowledge power as the main barrier to knowledge sharing within the organization. In

Table 3.2 General view analysis of selected studies

Author/year	*Study aims/objectives*	*Methodology*	*Main findings*	*Type of publication*
Abzari, Barzaki, and Abbasi (2011)	To study the effects of reputation enhancement and the loss of perceived knowledge power on the components of the reasoned action model, in order to analyze the behavior of knowledge sharing among employees of the agricultural bank in the state of Fars (Iran)	Survey with questionnaire to managers and experts of agricultural bank in Fars state; data analyzed applying structural equation modeling tool, Amos 15	This study provides evidence of two factors that managers should face when trying to encourage the sharing of organizational knowledge: that attitude has a direct impact on behavioral intention; and it also has a direct effect on knowledge sharing behavior	Original Article, *International Journal of Business and Social Science*, Center for Promoting Ideas (CPI), USA
Holland (2010)	Examine to what extent individual bank outcomes may be associated with lack of banking knowledge about the primary risks and value factors of their organizations by board directors and banking management	Development of a framework to understand the role of knowledge in banking based on a review of theoretical, empirical and historical literature on banking models, and analysis of bankruptcy and non-bankruptcy cases	Although the knowledge necessary for effective intermediation and management of banking risks is available, it has not been applied by banks, and this attitude has led several banks to bankruptcy	Original Article, *Journal of Financial Regulation and Compliance*, Emerald

(continued)

Table 3.2 (continued)

Author/year	*Study aims/objectives*	*Methodology*	*Main findings*	*Type of publication*
Kubo, Saka, and Pan (2001)	To understand how interactions between knowledge sharing, long-term relationships, human resource management practices and the role of social networks in one of Japan's commercial bank could mitigate possible knowledge loss	A qualitative, retrospective approach. The research is based on a single case study, employing unstructured interviews with bankers	The case of the Michiko bank demonstrates that the safety and commitment of work through full-time employees and a formalized job rotation allow the main employees to share experiences that constitute tacit knowledge and arouse the enthusiasm and willingness to exchange information and avoid knowledge loss	Original Article, *Human Resource Development International*, Taylor & Francis
Huang and Davison (2008)	Identify possible barriers to knowledge sharing within the bank in China	Single case study; face-to-face interviews to managers of the bank	Loss of knowledge power represents a critical barrier to knowledge sharing within the bank. Nonetheless, no particular negative impacts emerged from the interviews with the bankers	Conference Proceedings

Author/year	*Study aims/objectives*	*Methodology*	*Main findings*	*Type of publication*
Mohlala, Goldman, and Goosen (2012)	Understand the challenges faced in attracting and retaining IT professionals and how this can serve as an input to reduce the lack of skills and knowledge loss in the Information Technology divisions in a South Africa Bank	Case study; semi-structured interviews; Creshwell four stage data analysis process	The results indicate that employee turnover is the main contributor to skills shortages within the division studied. There is a lack of a retention strategy, also the organizational climate does not seem to be conducive to knowledge retention practices	Original Article, *Journal of Human Resource Management*, *SA Journal of Human Resource Management*

(continued)

Table 3.2 (continued)

Author/year	*Study aims/objectives*	*Methodology*	*Main findings*	*Type of publication*
Hogan and Manish (2016)	Demonstrate that Basel's RBC regulatory system is an excellent example of Hayekian's knowledge problem, and that the contextual, tacit and subjective knowledge required to correctly assess capital risk cannot be aggregated and used by regulators. Therefore, banking regulation must recognize man's limited knowledge and attach greater value to individual decisions than top-down planning	Application of Hayek's theory of knowledge to problems inherent to banking regulation	Regulators lack the knowledge required to carefully assess the risks of default and liquidity of securities, the risks of insolvency of individual banks and systemic risk in the global banking system	Original Article, *Advances in Austrian Economics*, Emerald

Author/year	*Study aims/objectives*	*Methodology*	*Main findings*	*Type of publication*
Shujahat et al. (2020)	Investigate if and how two-Tier HRM structures expose organizations to knowledge risks, both on-the-job, both during and after the turnover. Explore the attention of organizations to knowledge risks and the strategies that may be put into practice for their mitigation	Exploratory interviews with the six managers of six distinct Pakistan's private banks	There have been potential knowledge risks such as more critical on-the-job knowledge hoarding and hiding; while knowledge loss and leakage during and after turnover	Book Chapter
Tsang and Lee (2020)	Present and explain a methodology to identify the various knowledge risks for a preliminary assessment; present the Evidential Reasoning (ER) approach to improve the results obtained from traditional surveys on knowledge risks; illustrate the ER approach using a hypothetical example involving a bank	ER methodology illustrated with a hypothetical knowledge risk hierarchy of a bank	There are benefits from the application of the ER methodology	Book Chapter

(continued)

Table 3.2 (continued)

Author/year	*Study aims/objectives*	*Methodology*	*Main findings*	*Type of publication*
Glaser (2020)	To create a better understanding and improve awareness to knowledge risks, giving an overview of the knowledge risk management in leasing companies in Germany	In-depth expert interviews with chief risk officers or (owner-) managers including brief background information	The KRM framework presented should support leasing companies in the implementation of traditional risk management also considering knowledge risks	Book Chapter
Saringianni et al. (2015)	Find out if the risks arising from the use of social media highlighted in the literature also concern financial institutions. And if so, what strategies are implemented by financial institutions to deal with these risks	Semi-structured with twelve employees from ten different European financial institutions	Three major knowledge risks induced by social media were identified: difficulties of financial institutions to control the use of social media; lack of awareness of the use of social media; and huge spread of the impact of fake news that can go viral	Original article, *International Journal of Knowledge Management*
La Torre (2015)	To review some training evaluation models for anti-money laundering (AML) in banks, to figure out which would be most effective in preventing knowledge loss	Deductive approach to obtaining information from extant literature over the years engaged in study and criticism of training evaluation models	AML training evaluation model most effective to reduce the risk of knowledge loss and increase knowledge retention is the result of a mix of the characteristics of the models analyzed in the study	Conference Proceedings

Author/year	*Study aims/objectives*	*Methodology*	*Main findings*	*Type of publication*
La Torre (2018)	Contribute in diffusing practice of training evaluation in banks with specific reference to anti-money laundering issue	Semi-structured in-depth interview to a Board Chairman of an Italian bank	The interview shows the full willingness of the bank president to undertake AML training evaluation processes in the organization	Conference Proceedings

Source Our elaboration

particular, Abzari et al. (2011) underlined the importance of the attitude for encouraging knowledge sharing, which has a direct impact on behavioral intentions, could also influence knowledge sharing behavior. According to Kubo et al. (2001), an effective solution for knowledge loss, and to promote knowledge sharing, came from the creation of a secure organizational climate characterized by long-term (full-time job) and formalized working relationships, so that the employees, feeling confident, shared experiences deriving from their tacit knowledge. Also according to Shujahat, Akhtar, Nawaz, Wang, and Sumbal (2020) potential knowledge risks could occur in the context of working relationships, which could make knowledge sharing complicated; in particular, the authors identified knowledge hiding and knowledge hoarding as the main on-the-job knowledge risk, while turnover would be more exposed to knowledge loss risk both during and after it.

Four of analyzed studies proposed insights into the thematic area related to the lack of skills, or difficulties in general to manage knowledge risks. Among these, Holland (2010) associated the bankruptcies underlying the global financial crisis with a substantial inability of banking management to use the available knowledge. Mohlala et al. (2012), on the other hand, associated skills shortages to address knowledge risks to the turnover, which created a climate not conducive to the development of valid knowledge retention strategies. Hogan and Manish (2016) found the lack of adequate skills to a correct knowledge use in banks' regulators, which lack the knowledge necessary to assess the typical banking risks in the most correct way. According to Saringianni et al. (2015), pitfalls could be found in the difficulty of financial institutions to control the use of social networks in the organization; according to the authors, the difficulties in controlling the use, and especially the consequences of using social networks, could expose the organization to knowledge risks.

The thematic area relating to the proposals of frameworks or methods for KRM was covered by four of the studies analyzed. In the first, Tsang and Lee (2020) presented a methodology for knowledge risks identification based on the Evidential Reasoning (ER) approach, claiming that this approach could be supportive of traditional surveys methods, allowing to overcome possible critical issues typical of survey methods, such as the possibility that respondents base their responses on perceptions, insufficient information, and inaccurate facts. Also Glaser (2020), reporting the specific experience of the German leasing companies, contributed to spreading this experience to the other companies of the same sector that are facing the knowledge risks. La Torre (2015, 2018), proposed to act on the training of banking staff to better manage knowledge risks. In particular, the author underlined the importance of valuation of anti-money laundering training, suggesting a model deriving from a mix of the characteristics of training evaluation models provided by the reference literature.

Although not all the studies included in this review clearly identified the technical name of knowledge risks, and despite this review may not have provided a complete coverage of all empirical research in the field of KRM in banking and financial sectors, to the best of the authors' knowledge, no systematic review on this topic has previously been conducted. This could be a valid starting point to develop a line of research that explicitly deals with knowledge risks that could affect banks and other financial intermediaries of all sizes, typologies, and geographic origin.

References

Abzari, M., Barzaki, A. S., & Abbasi, R. (2011). Knowledge sharing behavior: Organizational reputation or losing organizational power case study: Employees of agricultural bank in Fars state. *International Journal of Business and Social Science*, *2*(17), 144–149.

Alavi, H. (2017). Risk management techniques and their application to documentary discrepancy in letter of credit transaction. *European Journal of Economic Studies, 6*, 4–17.

Ali, H. M., & Ahmad, N. H. (2006). Knowledge management in Malaysian banks: A new paradigm. *Journal of Knowledge Management Practice, 7*(3), 1–13.

Alrawi, K., & Elkhatib, S. (2009). Knowledge management practices in the banking industry: Present and future state-case study. *Journal of Knowledge Management Practice, 10*(4), 68–84.

Anagnostopoulos, Y., & Kabeega, J. (2018). Insider perspectives on European banking challenges in the post-crisis regulation environment. *Journal of Banking Regulation*, OnlineFirst, 1–23.

Aven, T. (2010). On how to define, understand and describe risk. *Reliability Engineering and System Safety, 95*(6), 623–631.

BCBS. (2008). *Principles for sound liquidity risk management and supervision.* Basel Committee on Banking Supervision. Switzerland: Bank for International Settlements.

BCE. (2018). *Guida della BCE sul processo interno di valutazione dell'adeguatezza patrimoniale (ICAAP).*

Birindelli, G., & Ferretti P. (2017). The operational risk: An overall framework. In *Operational risk management in banks*. Palgrave Macmillan Studies in Banking and Financial Institutions. London: Palgrave Macmillan.

Bratianu, C. (2018, July). *Hannibal ante portas and the knowledge risk framework*. In Proceedings of the 13th International Forum on Knowledge Asset Dynamics, Delft University of Technology, Delft, Netherlands (pp. 25–35).

Butzbach, O. K. E. (2014). *Alternative banking and financial crisis*. London: Pickering & Chatto.

Calder, A., & Watkins, S. (2010). *Risk Management: In information security risk management* for ISO27001/ISO27002 (pp. 42–53). IT Governance Publishing. Retrieved from www.jstor.org/stable/j.ctt5hh7jd.7.

Callahan, C., & Soileau, J. (2017). Does enterprise risk management enhance operating performance? *Advances in Accounting, 37,* 122–139.

Campanella, F., Derhy, A., & Gangi, F. (2019). Knowledge management and value creation in the post-crisis banking system. *Journal of Knowledge Management, 23*(2), 263–278.

Carretta, A., Fiordelisi, F., & Schwizer, P. (2017). *Risk culture in banking*. Springer International Publishing.

Cerchione, R., & Esposito, E. (2016). A systematic review of supply chain knowledge management research: State of the art and research opportunities. *International Journal of Production Economics, 182,* 276–292.

Chaikovska, I. (2019). *Implementation and effects of the post-crisis banking regulations in European Union*. Economic and Social Development: Book of Proceedings, 212–220.

Cham, T., Lim, Y., Cheng, B., & Lee, T. (2016). Determinants of knowledge management systems success in the banking industry. *VINE Journal of Information and Knowledge Management Systems, 46*(1), 2–20.

Corigliano, R. (2004). *L'intermediazione finanziaria,. Rischi e Controlli*. Bononia University Press.

Critical Appraisal Skills Programme. (2018). *CASP systematic review checklist*. Available at https://casp-uk.net/casp-tools-checklists/.

Cross, R., & Weller, S. (2001). Winning through knowledge (knowledge management in banks). *Financial World*, 19.

Curado, C. (2008). Perceptions of knowledge management and intellectual capital in the banking industry. *Journal of Knowledge Management, 12*(3), 141–155.

Dinesen, C. (2020). *Absent management in banking: How banks fail and cause financial crisis*. Berlin: Springer Nature.

Do Rosário Cabrita, M., & Vaz, J. L. (2005). Intellectual capital and value creation: Evidence from the Portuguese banking industry. *Electronic Journal of Knowledge Management, 4*(1), 11–20.

Durst, S., Bruns, G., & Henschel, T. (2016). The management of knowledge risks: What do we really know? In *Global business expansion: Concepts, methodologies, tools, and applications* (pp. 258–269). Hershey: IGI Global.

Durst, S., & Ferenhof, H. A. (2016). Knowledge risk management in turbulent times. *Competitive strategies for small and medium enterprises* (pp. 195–209). Cham: Springer.

Durst, S., & Henschel, T. (2020). *Knowledge Risk Management: From Theory to Praxis*. Berlin: Springer.

Durst, S., Hinteregger, C., & Zięba, M. (2019). The linkage between knowledge risk management and organizational performance. *Journal of Business Research, 105,* 1–10.

Durst, S., & Zięba, M. (2017). Knowledge risks-towards a taxonomy. *International Journal of Business Environment, 9*(1), 51–63.

Durst, S., & Zięba, M. (2018). Mapping knowledge risks: Towards a better understanding of knowledge management. *Knowledge Management Research & Practice, 17*(1), 1–13.

Edvardsson, R. I., & Durst, S. (2014). Outsourcing of knowledge processes: A literature review. *Journal of Knowledge Management, 18*(4), 795–811.

FSB. (2013). *Principles for an effective risk appetite framework.* Available at www.fsb.org.

Geretto, E. F., & Pauluzzo, R. (2015, September). *Knowledge management and risk culture in the banking industry: Relations and problems.* In European conference on knowledge management. Academic Conferences International Limited.

Glaser, C. (2020). Knowledge Risk Management in German leasing companies. In *Knowledge Risk Management* (pp. 159–183). Cham: Springer.

Gordon, L. A., Loeb, M. P., & Tseng, C. Y. (2009). Enterprise risk management and firm performance: A contingency perspective. *Journal of Accounting and Public Policy, 28*(4), 301–327.

Hogan, T. L., & Manish, G. P. (2016). Banking regulation and knowledge problems. *Advances in Austrian Economics, 20,* 213–234.

Holland, J. (2010). Banks, knowledge and crisis: A case of knowledge and learning failure. *Journal of Financial Regulation and Compliance, 18*(2), 87–105.

Huang, Q., & Davison, R. (2008). *Knowledge sharing barriers at the individual level in a Chinese bank.* PACIS 2008 Proceedings, 150.

Hung, Y. H., & Chou, S. C. (2005, August). *On constructing a knowledge management pyramid model.* In IRI-2005 IEEE International Conference on Information Reuse and Integration, Conf, 2005. (pp. 1–6). IEEE.

IDC. (2000). *Document synopsis. Implementation strategies for Knowledge Management in banking*; Part 2: "Analysis of Competition" [Online]. http://www.idc.com.

Irjayanti, M., & Azis, A. M. (2013). Knowledge Management for banking industry continuous improvement. *Sains Humanika, 64*(3), 55–59.

Jayasundara, C. C. (2008). Knowledge Management in banking industries: Uses and opportunities. *Journal of the University Librarians Association of Sri Lanka, 12*, 68–84.

Jesson, J., Matheson, L., & Lacey, F. M. (2011). *Doing your literature review: Traditional and systematic techniques*. Newcastle upon Tyne: Sage.

Khodadadyan, A., Mythen, G., Assa, H., & Bishop, B. (2018). Tools and techniques in risk assessment in Public Risk Management organisations. *International Journal of Economics and Management Engineering, 12*(10), 1277–1283.

Koh, E. H. (2019). *Risk management competency development in banks: An integrated approach*. Berlin: Springer.

Kokobe, S. A., & Gemechu, D. (2016). Risk management techniques and financial performance of insurance companies. *International Journal of Accounting Research, 4*(1), 126–127.

Kridan, B. A., & Goulding, S. J. (2006). A case study on knowledge management implementation in the banking sector. *VINE, 36*(2), 211–222.

Kubo, I., Saka, A., & Pan, S. L. (2001). Behind the scenes of knowledge sharing in a Japanese bank. *Human Resource Development International, 4*(4), 465–485.

La Torre, M. (2015). *The importance of knowledge retention in combating money laundering: Training evaluation as knowledge leakage prevention in banks*. IFKAD 2015 Proceedings. ISBN 978-88-96687-07-9; ISSN 2280-787X.

La Torre, M. (2018). *Know to fight:. The importance of non-wasting knowledge against money laundering. Evidence from an Italian bank*. IFKAD 2018 Proceedings. ISBN 978-88-96687-11-6; ISSN 2280-787X.

Laurens, F. (2012). Basel III and prudent risk management in banking: Continuing the cycle of fixing past crises. *Risk Governance & Control: Financial Markets & Institutions, 2*(3), 17–22.

Leo, M., Sharma, S., & Maddulety, K. (2019). Machine learning in banking risk management: A literature review. *Risks, 7*(1), 29.

Li, R. Y. M. (2013). Knowledge management, sharing and creation in developing countries' banking industries. *Advances in Network and Communications, 1*(1), 13–26.

Massingham, P., & Massingham, R. (2014). Does knowledge management produce practical outcomes? *Journal of Knowledge Management, 18*(2), 221–254.

McNamara, C. M.; Wedow, M., & Metrick, A. (2019). Basel III B: Basel III overview. *Journal of Financial Crises, 1*(4), 59–69. Available at https://elischolar.library.yale.edu/journal-of-financial-crises/vol1/iss4/4.

Moher, D., Liberati, A., Tetzlaff, J., Altman, D. G., & Prisma Group. (2009). Reprint—Preferred reporting items for systematic reviews and meta-analyses: The PRISMA statement. *Physical Therapy, 89*(9), 873–880.

Mohlala, J., Goldman, G. A., & Goosen, X. (2012). Employee retention within the information technology division of a South African bank. *SA Journal of Human Resource Management, 10*(2), 1–11.

Mongiardino, A., & Plath, C. (2010). Risk governance at large banks: Have any lessons been learned? *Journal of Risk Management in Financial Institutions, 3,* 116–123.

Moosakhani, M., Haghighi, M., & Torkzadeh, S. (2012). A model of gaining customer loyalty through customer knowledge management in banking industry of Iran (Private Banks). *Iranian Business Management, 4*(12), 147–164.

Nattapol, N., Peter, R., & Laddawan, K. (2010). An investigation of the determinants of knowledge management systems success in banking industry. *World Academy of Science, Engineering and Technology, 71*(1), 588–595.

Nurdin, N., & Yusuf, K. (2020). Knowledge management lifecycle in Islamic bank: The case of Syariah banks in Indonesia. *International Journal of Knowledge Management Studies, 11*(1), 59–80.

Ostrom, L. T., & Wilhelmsen, C. A. (2019). *Risk assessment: Tools, techniques, and their applications.* Hoboken: Wiley.

Pasha, M., Qaiser, G., & Pasha, U. (2018). A critical analysis of software risk management techniques in large scale systems. *IEEE Access, 6,* 12412–12424.

Petticrew, M., & Roberts, H. (2008). *Systematic reviews in the social sciences: A practical guide.* Hoboken: Wiley.

Pons, A. G., Lezama, O. B. P., Izquierdo, N. V., Herrera, H. H., & Silva, J. (2020). Influence of Knowledge Management between the bank and the local socioeconomic development: Correlational analysis. In *Proceedings of 6th International Conference on Big Data and Cloud Computing Challenges* (pp. 87–103). Singapore: Springer.

Quang, N. T. T., & Gan, C. (2019). Bank Risk Management: A regulatory perspective. In *Perspectives on risk, assessment and management paradigms.* IntechOpen.

Rashed, M. S. (2016). The readiness of banks in Knowledge Management: A study of three private commercial banks in Bangladesh. *Journal of Business & Financial Affairs, 5,* 181.

Rezaee, F., & Jafari, M. (2015). The effect of marketing knowledge management on sustainable competitive advantage: Evidence from banking industry. *Accounting, 1*(2), 69–88.

Rostami, A. (2016). Tools and techniques in risk identification: A research within SMEs in the UK construction industry. *Universal Journal of Management, 4*(4), 203–210.

Saringianni, C., Thalmann, S., & Manhart, M. (2015). Knowledge risks of social media in the financial industry. *International Journal of Knowledge Management (IJKM), 11*(4), 19–34.

Schiuma, G. (2012). Managing knowledge for business performance improvement. *Journal of Knowledge Management, 16*(4), 515–522.

Shad, M. K., Lai, F. W., Fatt, C. L., Klemeš, J. J., & Bokhari, A. (2019). Integrating sustainability reporting into enterprise risk management and its relationship with business performance: A conceptual framework. *Journal of Cleaner Production, 208,* 415–425.

Sheedy, E., & Lubojanski, M. (2018). Risk management behaviour in banking. *Managerial Finance, 44*(7), 902–918.

Shujahat, M., Akhtar, A., Nawaz, F., Wang, M., & Sumbal, M. S. (2020). Knowledge Risk Management in two-tier HRM structures. *Knowledge Risk Management* (pp. 49–68). Cham: Springer.

Smallman, C. (1999). Knowledge Management as risk management: A need for open governance? *Risk Management, 1*(4), 7–20.

Soltanizadeh, S., Rasid, S. Z. A., Golshan, N. M., & Ismail, W. K. W. (2016). Business strategy, enterprise risk management and organizational performance. *Management Research Review, 39*(9), 1016–1033.

Sorrentino, M. (1999, September). Notes on knowledge management in banking. In KIO Meeting, Barcelona: Spain [Online]. Available at http://www.sistemi-informativi.org/kio/cons/KIOme&BarRTF.htm.

Srinivasan, L. (2019). Operational Risk Management in banks—Measures for mitigation. *Vinimaya, 40*(1), 48–52.

Taherparvar, N. (2014). Customer knowledge management, innovation capability and business performance: A case study of the banking industry. *Journal of Knowledge Management, 18*(3), 591–610.

Tsang, H. W. C., & Lee, W. B. (2020). An integrated research methodology to identify and assess knowledge risk in a corporation with application to a financial institution. In *Knowledge risk management* (pp. 135–158). Cham: Springer.

Vasvári, T. (2015). Risk, risk perception, risk management—A review of the literature. *Public Finance Quarterly, 60*(1), 29–48.

Ward, R., Usher-Smith, J., & Griffin, S. (2019). How to produce a systematic review. *InnovAiT: Education and Inspiration for General Practice, 12*(3), 155–157.

Yamagata, K. (2002). *Knowledge management in banking industry: Comparative analysis between US and Japan* (Doctoral dissertation, Massachusetts Institute of Technology).

Zack, M., McKeen, J., & Singh, S. (2009). Knowledge management and organizational performance: An exploratory analysis. *Journal of Knowledge Management, 13*(6), 392–409.

CHAPTER 4

Does "Diversity" Make the Difference? Moving Inside the Sample

Abstract Business model based on proximity to the local community, direct relationships with customers, mutuality, cooperation, in one word "diversity". This chapter is aimed to provide an insight into the sample of cooperative banks involved in the case study in this book proposed, namely the "*Federazione delle Banche di Credito Cooperativo dell'Abruzzo e del Molise (Fedam)*". The analysis of the sample of Fedam cooperative banks is done through the testimony of the president of the board of directors of one of these banks, so as to understand their daily problems in a constantly changing context. In addition, an overview of the Italian Cooperative Credit System is also provided, and a digression on the concept of diversity in banking is presented as well, aiming to consider whether diversity could make the difference or not for Cooperative Credit Banks (CCBs) in some different situations: during and after crisis; against the risk; and in governance. Nowadays, CCBs are facing important challenges in terms of efficiency, risk control, and corporate governance, and it could be useful to investigate whether diversity could represent an advantage or an obstacle in facing these and other challenges.

The section "The Italian Cooperative Credit System" is contributed by Michele Samuele Borgia.

M. La Torre, *Risk in Banking*,
https://doi.org/10.1007/978-3-030-54498-0_4

Keywords Diversity in banking · Mutuality · Cooperative Credit Banks · Italian Cooperative Credit System · Sample banks

4.1 Introduction

There may be several systemic benefits deriving from diversity of business models and ownership structures in the banking sector; for example, not being subject to short-term capital market pressures, which could lead banks to take excessive risks to the point of compromising their own stability. Cooperative banks benefit from this diversity, as their business model focuses on proximity to the local community and banking relationships, a "way of banking" that can also reduce the powerful centrifugal tendencies in the financial system (Ayadi, Llewellyn, Schmidt, Arbak, & Pieter De Groen, 2010). If there is a lesson that has been (or should be) learned, after the financial crisis, is that the role of cooperative banking should be reaffirmed, and its importance valued, an importance based on the unique ability to support real economy through providing credit to households and SMEs. The systemic importance of cooperative banks and their diversity should also be further assessed in "an emerging strand of literature aiming to demonstrate that diversity in banking can bring significant advantages in terms of financial stability, systemic risk management and easiness for the economy to respond to economic downturns" (Migliorelli, 2018, p. 232).

The aim of this chapter is to answer this call, providing an insight into the sample of cooperative banks involved in the case study presented in this book, namely, the *Federazione delle Banche di Credito Cooperativo dell'Abruzzo e del Molise (Fedam)*. After presenting a brief overview of the Italian Cooperative Credit System, useful for understanding the operational context of our sample of banks, the analysis deepened into daily problems of a CCB Fedam member through some reflections by the president of the board of directors on the problems that these banks face every day in a turbulent context. Before this part of the chapter, a digression on the concept of diversity in banking is proposed, considering whether diversity could make the difference or not for Cooperative Credit Banks (CCBs) in some different situations: diversity in times of crisis; diversity as protection from risk or cause of risk exposure; diversity in governance. Nowadays, CCBs are facing important challenges in terms of efficiency, risk control, and corporate governance, and it could be useful to investigate whether diversity that distinguishes them could in any way represent an advantage or an obstacle in facing these and other challenges.

For this purpose, the remainder of the chapter is structured as follows: in Sects. 4.2, 4.3, and 4.4 diversity in case of crisis, against the risk, and about the CCBs governance were, respectively, addressed. The chapter ends with Sect. 4.5, in which a brief overview of the Italian Cooperative Credit System was provided together with the direct contribution of an administrator of a CCBs who presented some personal reflections on the issues dealt with in the chapter as a whole.

4.2 Diversity Against the Crisis

"Cooperation is a crucial behavioral principle of human social life, and it is key to our survivorship." Cornée, Fattobene, and Migliorelli (2018) quoted this phrase to introduce the concept of cooperation and advantages that could be drawn from it. Several benefits, indeed, could be attributed to the economic cooperation. For example, cooperation allows to quantitatively improve the resource production capabilities; moreover, allows to increase variety and quantity of goods and services individuals can acquire; and could also represent a protection from the environment's turbulence. Even in banking sector, cooperation could bring greater benefits. It is no coincidence, in fact, that cooperative banks demonstrated a particular adaptability to the challenges imposed by the global financial crisis. Only in some cases government support was necessary, remaining these banks for the most part profitable thanks to their localism, allowing this to better control risks associated with local businesses relationship (Meyer, 2018). In Italy, for example, during the two financial crises, the US subprime of 2007–2009 and the euro-originated sovereign of 2010–2012, credit cooperative banks (CCBs), like all local banks, gained increasing weight in the financing of families and businesses; in fact, reversing the trend of the rest of the system, between 2007 and 2014, CCBs expanded their territorial network, which included about a quarter of the bank branches in the area. Throughout this period, cooperative banks presented growth rates of loans to the private sector higher than those of the other banks, with particularly wide gaps in the two-year period 2008–2009, when they benefited from a structurally more limited funding gap and collection constraints on smaller international markets compared to large banks (Stefani et al., 2016). Also at international level, cooperative banks maintained a higher incidence of loans on total assets compared to other banks even in the period of crisis, with a positive effect on the growth of added value in the manufacturing sector and in those most dependent on external finance (Becchetti, Ciciretti, & Paolantonio, 2014); these banks "charged a higher spread before the crisis, offered more favorable continuation-lending terms in response to the crisis, and suffered fewer defaults" (Bolton, Freixas,Gambacorta, & Mistrulli, 2013, p. 1). Therefore, lending behavior of cooperative banks seems to be the key element of "banking diversity" that should deserve particular attention in order to understand the effective ability of these banks to play significant countercyclical role. Analyzing the lending behavior of CCBs could also offer the possibility of highlighting strengths and weaknesses of their business model in periods of economic and financial stress, also reasoning on eventual improvement solutions. In this regard, a recent study aimed at verifying whether the traditional cooperative banks countercyclical role can be confirmed or has to be questioned, albeit verifying that the countercyclical role of cooperative banks can be confirmed for the entire north-eastern half of the euro area, but not equally as regards the south-western half of the continent—hit more severely by the crisis—highlighted the intrinsic attitude of cooperative banks to be financial actors strongly anchored to the real economy at the local level, confirming that the medium-term ability to ensure satisfactory economic performance seems to be a crucial condition for sustaining their unique business model and for providing distinctive value to members and to society (Migliorelli, 2018).

So can we speak of a special ability of CCBs to overcome crises? Cooperative banks are really those "frontier operators that bring banking services where otherwise would not have arrived, supporting individual entrepreneurial initiatives, and favoring the economic development of communities? Nevertheless, and perhaps contrary to popular opinion, in their habitat this banks denote a greater ability to provide credit than other banks" (Padoa-Schioppa, 1996).

4.3 Diversity Against the Risk

Research on the risks of cooperative banks, to date, still seems relatively thin, and mainly focused on credit risk. In fact, some of the most recent studies on risk exposure and management of cooperative banks, refer to a strand rather fragmented and poor in contributions; and this is already evident from the fact that in these works more often reference is made to retail banking rather than specifically to cooperatives or mutual banking (Mare & Gramlich, 2020).

Mare and Gramlich (2020), while stating that only few studies systematically address risk exposure and risk management in the cooperative banking sector, contributed to the literature by investigating the risk exposure of cooperative banks in Austria, Germany, and Italy, and in particular by observing whether there are similarities in the risk characteristics for specific groups of cooperative banks, also highlighting how important is, from a systemic point of view, to know to what extent there is a common or different risk profile of the entities that indicates a potential for diversification within the cooperative banking system.

In other works (Soana & Ferri, 2019), it was shown how changes in the governance of small cooperative banks deriving from the remuneration rules introduced by Directive 2013/36/EU (CRD-IV) were not clearly associated with risk exposure. To deepen understanding of how cooperative banks recently deal with risk, Caldarelli, Fiondella, Maffei, and Zagaria (2016) highlighted, instead, Enterprise Risk Management (ERM) practices enabling dual-purpose organizations to manage the risks associated with a duality of purpose. Cattaneo and Bassani (2019) then highlighted the factors that could facilitate the integration between Enterprise Risk Management (ERM) and Management Accounting Systems (MAS) in small financial contexts such as Italian cooperative credit banks, investigating how strategic and operational decision-making changes in light of this integration. Balina and Nowak (2017) proposed a model that could support cooperative banks in reducing the risk associated with loans to individual customers, identifying with precision almost all the so-called "bad customers" through some variables describing loan applicants (age, higher education, current loans, maximum number of defaults on the payment due) which, linked to the assessment of the regressive ratios, returned a highly effective credit risk indicator for identifying potentially insolvent clients. Other studies analyzed cyber risk management in cooperative banks, trying to fill the gap in understanding considering this type of risk and its management as an integral part of business management (Ossola, Giovando, & Crovini, 2017). D'Amato (2018), on the other hand, tried to directly correlate the difference in risk-taking between cooperative banks and joint stock banks to banking governance and, in particular, to board characteristics; such an investigation could add new evidence to the ongoing debate, very active in Europe, on what the aforementioned differences should be in terms of business concepts and business models, and on how these differences should be reflected in both banking regulation and corporate governance standards. In Sahut and Bouheni (2019), the effect of economic growth and liberalization on cooperative banks' risk-taking was investigated, arguing that cooperative banks have relatively higher financial stability with relatively less risk-taking than other banks: indeed, by forming a subset of shareholder-value-banks, cooperative banks tend to have less propensity to take risks than shareholder-value-banks. In the end, with specific reference to the Italian Cooperative Banking System, the Iccrea Group, established with Law no. 49 of 2016 (see below Sect. 4.5), classified as "significant" since 2014, and therefore included in the European Central Bank's range of supervision and subject to specific prudential supervisory processes, during 2018, was involved in a project in the risk management area aimed at evolving and integrating the operational and IT risk management frameworks; this revision, ensuring regulatory compliance, also enables the management component of aforementioned frameworks to pay particular attention to the identification of automation solutions (Badaluccio, 2019).

From the brief review conducted in this Section, a rather disjointed picture of the most recent studies on risk management of cooperative banks emerges. There does not seem to be a well-defined line of research, but there is nevertheless a growing interest of scholars in this topic. Every aspect of the possible influence of cooperative banks' diversity on risk management should deserve further investigation, both to understand in depth whether and how this diversity in banking may affect risk exposure, and to identify new and more effective risk controls in an environment in continuous evolution and characterized by the technological progress of financial systems.

4.4 Diversity and the Governance

"When you ask a member of any cooperative bank what it is that makes the cooperative model unique, the immediate answer is: governance." With these words, Lamarque (2018, p. 141) underlined the importance of governance in such a particular banking system as the cooperative one. While citing features actually making cooperative credit system "a model of democracy" (members are the owners of the cooperatives; each member has only one right voting, regardless of the amount of money invested in shares), the author pointed out, at the same time, that in reality there is not always a great deal of attention to what it means to be an active member, either because of the lack of effective willingness to participate, or sometimes because of the forgetfulness of owning a share, or because only the return on investment counts. However, given reputational damage that banking system in general suffered due to its responsibilities in the global financial crisis, cooperative banks are currently rediscovering the importance of membership, but even more, the importance to have an effective and responsible governance to rely on. The question at this point could be "How are financial cooperatives governed? This seemingly simple question is of great importance, because beyond their unique status and shared democratic principle of one member-one vote, cooperatives exhibit a diverse spectrum of complex corporate governance strategies, and decision-making is the result of dynamic interactions between organizational levels and managerial and policy structures" (Deville & Lamarque, 2015, p. 2). In this regard, it could be argued that diversity characterizing cooperative banks' governance could generate "untouchable" directors hardly replaceable and, therefore, free to act in a kind of self-referential way. Despite there might be some truth in this statement, one should not overlook the possibility that the long term of cooperative banks' administrators could represent the inevitable "price to pay" to allow a wider stakeholders' representation: thanks to the greater stability of the administrators, cooperative banks are better able to pursue long-term objectives (Ferri, 2012). In these terms, it would be more appropriate to consider the challenges that diversity poses to cooperative banks, starting from the relationship with regulatory context (in particular the latest Recommendations on the principles of business governance for the banking sector by the Basel Committee on Banking Supervision of July 2015), that engenders several challenges about governance, with particular reference to recruitment, tasks and remuneration, and to periodic evaluation of board members. In all these cases, the real challenge will be to seek new solutions and tools capable of both maintaining the peculiarities of the cooperative model, and of constituting a board with the characteristics of financial and technical skills required by regulation (Lamarque, 2018).

In any case, one cannot fail to consider that basically "good governance" largely depends on the behavior of individuals and, in this field, cooperative banks undoubtedly have a great advantage. Indeed, cooperative values focusing on transparency, responsibility, solidarity, and sustainability, confer to bank directors a "particular ethic, guiding them towards behaviour less conducive to financial failures. Board members have a stewardship role, a responsibility towards members to leave the bank in better shape than they found it" (EACB, 2016, p. 6).

4.5 The Italian Cooperative Credit System

(Michele Samuele Borgia)

4.5.1 Origins, Evolution, Reforms: A Brief Overview

The movement of cooperative banks spread throughout most of continental Europe since the second half of the nineteenth century, in a historical period in which banks activities were limited to urban areas serving only the wealthiest classes, while the emerging class of workers, composed of merchants and farmers with little or no collateral, had limited access to credit. "Charitable sources and public funds remained insufficient, credit obtained from money lenders was often available only at exorbitant interest rates: by and large, the birth of credit cooperatives in Europe was a response to the challenge of providing affordable loans to this emerging class" (Ayadi, Llewellyn, Schmidt, Arbak, & Pieter De Groen, 2010, p. 1). The development of nineteenth-century ideal of cooperation is based on the desire to make explicit the principle of society constitution, which was lost in the tumult of rapid and unceasing economic changes: "Co-operative ideal is a as old as human society. It is the idea of conflict and competition as a principle of economic progress that is new" (Carr-Saunders & Flawrence, 1938, p. 23).

In Italy, the presence of cooperative banking has a long tradition. At the end of the nineteenth century, critical economic conditions, especially in rural areas promoted new forms of financial support for small farmers and artisans, in response to the cyclical problems in the agricultural sector throughout Europe. In such a context, the first *Banca Popolare* (BP) was established in Lodi in 1864, following the example of the German *Volksbanken*, a model introduced in Italy through the studies of the economist Luigi Luzzatti (Di Salvo & Lopez, 2018); and thanks to the action of a German priest, FW Raiffeisen, strongly supported by the Catholic Church, the first *Cassa Rurale* (or *Banca Rurale, RB*) was established near Padua (Loreggia), in 1883 (Di Salvo & Lopez, 2010). Over the following years, both BPs and RBs underwent reform processes, which culminated with the reform of the RBs, in 1993, to achieve full compliance with the universal banking model introduced by the Second Banking Coordination Directive (89/646/EEC) and, on that occasion, were also renamed *Cooperative Credit Banks* (CCBs). Other important changes occurred, then, in 2015, with the reform of the BPs (Law n. 33/2015); and, in 2016, with the reform of the CCBs (Law n. 49/2016).

4.5.1.1 *The Experience of CCBs in Italy*

The Italian Consolidated Law on Banking (Legislative Decree 385/1993), in Article 28, establishes that "the exercise of banking activities by cooperative companies is reserved for popular banks and cooperative credit banks." Hence, the current model provides that Italian CCBs are subject to the same banking legislation and supervisory regulations as other banks, although with some additional restrictions: "at least from a legislative point of view, CCBs are firstly banks, and secondly cooperatives. Differently from other banks, their Statute plays a crucial role, since it translates into internal rules the supervisory regulation of the Bank of Italy" (Catturani & Stefani, 2016, pp. 150, 152). The CCBs legislative framework is aimed at the improvement of a financial intermediary dedicated to the economic and social development at local level, also exploiting scale-and scope- economies, so to improve cooperative movement's strength, through the improvement of product differentiation, economic efficiency, and thus competitiveness (Catturani & Stefani, 2016).

4.5.1.2 *Guiding Principles of CCBs*

"Cooperative credit banks that comply with the mutuality requirements set out in article 2514 of the civil code, and that exercise credit mainly in favor of the members, are considered as cooperatives with prevailing mutuality" (Legislative Decree 385/1993, Article 28, paragraph 2-bis). Beyond all changes and reforms followed over time, the Italian Consolidated Law on Banking always preserved the distinctive features of Italian Cooperative Credit Banks. mutualism, democracy, localism, and non-profit principles. Although these principles are common to all CCBs, "it is important to underline that these principles are often implemented differently from one cooperative bank to another, thus contributing to the sector's diversity" (Lamarque, 2018, p. 142).

CCBs' activity is guided by principle of mutualism. Mutuality is a specific way of doing business, a formula of organization and business management based on joining forces, building social capital, and establishing relationships based on reciprocity and cooperation. For CCBs, mutuality is a fundamental part of their identity. A distinctive value, enshrined in law and which pervades history, strategies, organizational models, but also the operating style. CCBs' mutuality, at the same time, is internal, aimed at bank members; external, directed to the local communities in which they operate; systemic, i.e., generated by the Cooperative Credit network system; and international, aimed at supporting the experience of the cooperative formula in other countries (Official Web Site of Italian Cooperative Credit).

CCBs' activity is guided by principle of democracy, according to which their customers can join as members. Each member is entitled to one vote regardless of the share of capital held and the amount of deposits and loans. During the assemblies, the role of the members is similar to that played by the shareholders in the traditional assemblies, to differentiate significantly is the "one member, one vote" rule: "In this respect, a long-term vision based on social engagement usually takes precedence over short-term financial needs and a large proportion of the economic results usually remains within the cooperative" (Lamarque, 2018, p. 143).

CCBs' activity is guided by principle of localism. On the basis of this principle, the CCBs encourage territorial strengthening by guaranteeing proximity to members and customers. Even the structure of these banks is organized according to this principle, thus respecting the territory and the history that characterizes it. The connection with the territory is such that the governance structure is often defined as an "inverse pyramid": "the local chairman of the board becomes a member of the board of the regional structure. And the chairman of the board at the regional level could be elected to the board of the national level. Ultimately, any local member could become the chairman of the board of a large cooperative banking group" (Lamarque, 2018, p. 145).

CCBs' activity is guided by the non-profit principle. Cooperative credit banks must allocate at least 70% of annual net profits to the legal reserve. A portion of the annual net profits must be paid to mutual funds for the promotion and development of cooperation to the extent and in the manner prescribed by law. The portion of profits that is not assigned pursuant to the preceding paragraphs and that is not used for the revaluation of the shares or assigned to other reserves or distributed to shareholders must be destined for charity or mutuality purposes (Art. 37, Banking Law).

4.5.1.3 Time to Reform

"Over time, cooperative banking model of the 'survivors' evolved and differentiated into a multiplicity of European institutions with characteristics reflecting the needs of cooperative members on the one hand and the specificities of national legislative frameworks on the other" (Groeneveld, 2014, p. 13). In the Italian banking system, cooperative credit currently occupies a prominent position, ranking third for the number of branches and fourth for the total number of loans; at the end of 2018, CCBs were present with over 4300 operating branches, equal to 16% of the national total; in over 90% of the Italian municipalities in which they operate, they represent the only financial intermediary (Bank of Italy, 2019). This prominent position, on the one hand, highlighted the positive role played by the CCBs in the banking sector but, on the other, brought to light possible weaknesses and inconsistencies in the cooperative model; these awareness, together with the implementation of the Banking Union at European level have probably created the conditions for a reform of the cooperative banking system in Italy (Di Salvo & Lopez, 2018). The Italian Cooperative Credit reform took place in 2016, through the Law 8 April 2016 n. 49 and its modifications. To fully understand the scope of this reform, it is necessary to keep in mind the context in which it was formulated. International rules underwent a marked tightening during the years of the crisis, for all banks, and therefore also for the CCBs, which however, unlike the other banks, were unable to raise capital on the market, or implement operational diversification strategies and territorial, due to the constraints due to the cooperative form. The reform is conceived precisely with the aim of overcoming these limits (Barbagallo, 2018). Following the system reform, Italian Cooperative Credit underwent profound structural changes with the introduction of the new figure of the *Cooperative Banking Groups*, in action since 2019. Over 260 Cooperative Credit Banks, Rural Banks and *Casse Raiffeisen* (Alto Adige) remain at the base of the entire italian cooperative system, keeping intact their characteristics of autonomous banks (with their own administrators elected by the respective social bases), mutual banks (providing credit mainly to shareholders), and local banks (with defined territorial operations). Despite this, the individual CCBs, under penalty of losing their banking license, are obliged by the reform law to join a *Cooperative Banking Group* (except for the Raiffeisen banks of South Tyrol which have had the option to opt for the creation of a IPS—Institutional Protection Scheme), and are in fact the owners of the new Cooperative Banking Groups (with at least 60% of the capital). This Cooperative

Groups, maintaining functions of direction and coordination, guarantee greater efficiency of the entire system, also in the prevention of possible critical situations, with the aim of continuing the original experience of bank mutuality. Some facts. The activity of the Banking Group *Cassa Centrale Banca*, based in Trento, started on 14 January 2019; 84 CCBs belong to this Group. On March 2019, the *Iccrea* Cooperative Banking Group, the largest Italian cooperative banking group, operating in Rome, formed by 142 Cooperative Credit Banks. The 39 *Raiffeisen banks* of South Tyrol, at the beginning of 2019, instead started the organizational phase that will lead to the establishment, in accordance with European legislation, of an IPS, *Institutional Protection Scheme*, that is, a form of cross-guarantee to protect the financial soundness of the participating banks and in order to prevent critical issues. The unitary representation of the system is instead ensured by *Federcasse*, the Italian Federation of Cooperative Credit Banks and Rural Banks, which ensures the representation of the category, managing the national collective labor contract for the over 35 thousand employees of Cooperative Credit, provides legal, fiscal, organizational and communication consultancy for the benefit of the 15 local Federations (Official Website of the Italian Cooperative Credit).

Despite the extraordinary scope of the reform, it could lead to collateral problems which in the long run could undermine the stability of the entire cooperative credit system. In this regard, a recent study analyzed the possible effects of the 2016 CCBs reform in terms of indirect enhancement of predatory finance; relational mechanisms between the parent company and the CCBs could limit the decision-making autonomy of the latter when granting loans. This possible limitation on access to legal sources of financing could indirectly increase the use of illicit channels showing the risk of usury for the companies involved (Barone, 2018).

4.5.1.4 *Time for Challenges*

What will remain of the mutualistic nature of credit cooperation? How the mutuality CCBs will be configured? How will the competitive regime change? How will the bank-customer relationship change? How will credit risk be managed at the level of individual CCBs? These are just some of the questions arising from the changes that the recent CCBs Reform required, starting with those originating from the need to modernize governance (Cardarelli, 2017). But other challenges await

Italian CCBs. First of all, those deriving from the Basel III Agreement. In a survey carried out on a large sample of Italian CCBs, a not fully efficient allocation of resources within the system was highlighted, especially with reference to short-term liquidity. If, on the one hand, the cooperative system seems to have widely available, and in full autonomy, the means necessary to comply with the new regulatory standards, it is equally evident that more functional management methods must be adopted, which allow to redistribute resources within the CCBs' network (Cannata et al., 2013). Although in recent years there has been increasing progress toward designing a regulatory framework that takes into due account the differences between financial institutions, much remains to be done to ensure that disproportionate regulatory barriers do not compromise the business model of cooperative banks and other similar institutions: "[...] the risk associated with a 'one-size-fits-all' approach to banking regulation is reduced competitiveness of smaller and less complex institutions like the majority of cooperative banks, with a potentially adverse impact in terms of their ability to continue to serve the local economy" (Caselli, 2018, p. 226). Other challenges for the Italian CCBs could also come from the process of digitization of organizational processes, which could require increasingly specialized and advanced professional profiles, and highlight gaps in already operational human resources.

Compared to such a scenario, and considering today's cooperative banking in the rest of Europe, the key to successfully facing challenges such as those posed by CCBs Reform could lie in the promotion of the so-called *financial inclusion*: "as social organizations, CCBs qualify as entities that originally and still now depend on their ability to create and give direction to communities. The basis of this power lay initially in their ability to allow people to participate in something that was more powerful than themselves and that enabled them to become financially and socially included" (Poli, 2019, p. 24).

4.5.2 *The Federazione delle Banche di Credito Cooperativo dell'abruzzo e del Molise: Reflections by an Administrator*

The purpose of this book is to outline a specific Knowledge Risk Management framework for cooperative credit banks. In this chapter, we wanted to take an overview of the Italian Credit Cooperative System, analyzing it through the characteristic that perhaps most distinguishes it, for better or for worse, namely, the diversity.

This Section closes the chapter considering the cooperative reality representing the sample of the empirical analysis presented in this work (see Chapter 5), that is a local Federation of CCBs, the *Federazione delle Banche di Credito Cooperativo dell'Abruzzo e del Molise (Fedam)*, which represents eight CCBs operating in the areas of competence. It was decided to do this through the words of those who administer one CCB Fedam member. In the Box 4.1, the reflections of the president of a CCBs that currently has to combine localism and belonging to an articulated and complex banking group.

Box 4.1 The direct experience of a CCB administrator

After ten years of studies in the economics of credit companies, in 2000, I accepted to join the board of statutory auditors of the Banca di Credito Cooperativo Abruzzese—Cappelle sul Tavo, in 2005 in the board of statutory auditors of the cooperative credit bank. Gambatesa and in 2006 that of the Cooperative Credit Bank of the Middle Adriatic. Since 2009 I have been elected President of the Board of Directors of the Banca di Credito Cooperativo Abruzzese—Cappelle sul Tavo.

It can be defined as a long and varied experience in a reality characterized by medium-small dimensions, with essential organizational structures and with knowledge training processes supported by the production of circulars and training activities carried out by the trade association (Federcasse), in its territorial structure, and by the continuous effort to transform the product of the regulatory supervision carried out by the Bank of Italy into operating systems suitable to face the growing systemic complexity.

I accepted with great pleasure the invitation sent by the author to participate in this study, because it represented a moment of reflection and self-diagnosis on the level of awareness of the role of strategic supervision and/or management.

Currently, cooperative credit banks, in Italy in particular, are becoming "significant" as being part of one of the largest banking groups in Italy, and being subjected to sudden and persistent operational standardization procedures and strategies, and to a system of controls of varied and articulated profiling.

One sensation prevails over all. At this time of historical changes for Italian cooperative credit, knowledge is not yet attributed an economic value, nor is it recognized as a strategic asset. In reality, if the value of knowledge and its degree of dissemination and engraftment within banking realities cannot be accounted for, the simple reading of bank balance sheets highlights the existence of managerial profiles of excellence or weakness, directly deriving from the levels of presence of knowledge in the overall structure of each bank. And it is much more than just clues, being able to easily clear the field of elements deriving from geo-environmental, technological, or socio-economic interferences thanks to the co-presence in the same markets of more or less performing benchmarks, that allow to identify, in the human component, the main driver for the achievement of the company's operating results.

Going further down to the micro-cosmos level of individual credit companies, the lack of homogeneity in the performances of the commercial structures highlights wide differential features attributable to the propensities and knowledge available to the human resources located in the structures. On the other hand, the pressure exerted by the regulatory provisions on pre-measures necessary to face the increasingly complex system of risks, has introduced elements of absorbent complexity in terms of strategic choices increasingly oriented towards cultivating adequate growth.

The elements of fragility and operational inadequacy ended up concentrating on the entrepreneurial profile of the bank organizations, also in relation to an ever applied principle of proportionality in the definition of functional paradigms to a risk management that unnaturally shifted the center of gravity of the overall management of the Institutes towards controls.

The greater part of the training plans adopted had, consequently, to be consistent with the gaps of knowledge of the "fulfillment" type with respect to the standards set by the primary and secondary legislative rain on controls and risk management. But the loss of coherence with the need for commercial strengthening and diversification of the capacity to offer banking and financial services and the consequent project deficit that the Institutes have unknowingly accumulated have resulted in the overall strategic-management activity, also in terms of production, allocation, management and development of a system of knowledge consistent with market opportunities which, in the meantime, generated the technical education of customers by virtue of the growth of exogenous knowledge to institutions. The inadequate knowledge of the organization as a whole or of its components has, therefore, made the strategies based on traditional forms of credit intermediation, characterized by profitability apparently performing during the economic cycles characterized by euphoria and a structural growth in risk appetite and absolutely insufficient to guarantee management balances on their own—even gross of the cost of risk and the cost of capital—in the recession.

The way identified to lighten the incidence of the cost of risk was to keep the gap between active and passive rates wide, given the good positioning in the internal areas, which up to now have been characterized by the presence of less demanding and less informed customers than system of prices requested by other size and positioning credit intermediaries for the offer of banking and financial services.

Nonetheless, the systemic compression of the spread between lending and lending rates has seriously undermined the earning opportunities that could lead to these position rents. With increasingly reduced margins from money management, specific risks of the financed subjects and systematic economic situation, for a long time, high—or very high—self-financing becomes difficult, a practice of particular strategic value in Institutes that on average, they do not have the possibility of accessing the official markets both for the chosen legal status and for more general economic evaluations. The repositioning has thus become an unavoidable choice, through a process of expansion and diversification of the offer of banking products and investment services whose articulation and competitiveness, must be able to stand comparison with that of banking realities dimensionally capable of achieving much more important economies of scale, where possible, by resorting to the pure marketing of quality services made by other product companies.

But to be convincing, in a context in which the offer of innovative financial services, moving on the net, manages to reach the customers on whom the aforementioned "position rents" have been experimented, as well as requesting the right attitudes emotional, it requires a deep knowledge of the markets, the products offered—even by competitors–and techniques for analyzing customer needs.

It is a challenge on which the larger banks have already been able to take advantage of it, benefiting from the lower incidence–even if they are considered significant banks—of the charges connected with the activation of the safeguards prescribed by current regulations. And the results can easily be seen from the reading of the financial statements of the latter, usually characterized by a lower specific weight of the interest margin on the brokerage margin and, in general, by a lower incidence of value adjustments on loans on the income formation.

A perspective that can lead to a reduction in the overall need for equity and to the easier achievement of higher capital requirements for the same absolute value of the bank's own funds. This is a test bench that will require a non-ordinary commitment in terms of redesigning the overall "mission" of the small institutions, which will have to try to mediate between the need not to settle in relation to the traditional clientele that has given proof of appreciating their ability to listen and monitor the territory and the prospect of having to turn the opportunities for contacting customers up to now valued in a predominantly "transactional" way.

Selling consultancy offers greater and less risky profit prospects than the sale of financial transactions with low or negative added value but requires a strategic requalification free from mechanistic approaches in which the vision of the overall system of knowledge of which the Organization has is very clear and will need, marking them, where possible, with respect to intertemporal horizons with career paths defined in accordance with the structural purposes that the bank must be able to achieve, with plans for the rotation of human resources that make corporate knowledge pass from individual to individual, editing redundancies and structural voids. Even the training courses will have to abandon the "fulfilling" approaches and orient themselves to precise strategies of "creation and diffusion" of those knowledge necessary to carry out process and product innovation which, perhaps, cannot avoid maturity or decline in the traditional credit sector of the traditional meaning but which will be able to support it in the indifferent evolution to which it must give way.

Source Our elaboration

References

Ayadi, R., Llewellyn, D. T., Schmidt, R. H., Arbak, E., & Pieter De Groen, W. (2010). Investigating diversity in the banking sector in Europe: Key developments, performance and role of cooperative banks (September 14, 2010). *CEPS Paperbacks*, September 2010. Available at SSRN: https://ssrn.com/abstract=1677335.

Badaluccio, G. (2019). *Iccrea sceglie Augeos. L'evoluzione del risk management*. Available on http://www.datamanager.it/2019/11/iccrea-sceglie-augeos-levoluzione-del-risk-management/.

Balina, R., & Nowak, M. (2017). Assessing individual credit risk on the basis of discriminant analysis by Poland's cooperative banks. *International Journal of Business Continuity and Risk Management, 7*(2), 103–112.

Banca d'Italia (2019). *Banche e istituzioni finanziarie: articolazione territoriale*. Statistiche. Available on www.bancaditalia.it.

Barbagallo, C. (2018). *La riforma delle Banche di Credito Cooperativo: presupposti e obiettivi*. Available on www.bancaditalia.it.

Barone, R. (2018). The Italian CCB reform and usury credit risk: A quantitative analysis. *Italian Economic Journal, 4*(3), 463–496.

Becchetti, L., Ciciretti, R., & Paolantonio, A. (2014). *Is there a cooperative bank difference?* (CEIS Tor Vergata Research Paper Series 313).

Bolton, P., Freixas, X., Gambacorta, L., & Mistrulli, P. E. (2013). *Relationship and transaction lending in a crisis* (Bank for International Settlements, Working Papers No. 417).

Caldarelli, A., Fiondella, C., Maffei, M., & Zagaria, C. (2016). Managing risk in credit cooperative banks: Lessons from a case study. *Management Accounting Research, 32,* 1–15.

Cannata, F., D'Acunto, G., Allegri, A., Bevilacqua, M., Chionsini, G., Lentini, T., ... & Trevisan, G. (2013). Il credito cooperativo alla sfida di Basilea 3: tendenze, impatti, prospettive (Italian Mutual Banks and the Challenge of Basel III). *Bank of Italy Occasional Paper*, (158).

Cardarelli, M. C. (Ed.). (2017). *Nuove opportunità e sfide per le banche di credito cooperativo: la riforma del 2016*. G Giappichelli Editore.

Carr-Saunders, A. M., & Flawrence, P. S. (1938). *Consumers' cooperation in Great Britain: An examination of the British co-operative movement*. London: George Allen and Unwin.

Caselli, G. (2018). The cooperative banks today in the EU perspective. In *New cooperative banking in Europe* (pp. 201–229). Cham: Palgrave Macmillan.

Cattaneo, C., & Bassani, G. (2019). *Enterprise risk management e management accounting systems in una Banca di Credito Cooperativo.* MANAGEMENT CONTROL.

Catturani, I., & Stefani, M. L. (2016). Italian credit cooperative banks. In *Credit cooperative institutions in European countries* (pp. 149–167). Cham: Springer.

Cornée, S., Fattobene, L., & Migliorelli, M. (2018). An overview of cooperative banking in Europe. In *New cooperative banking in Europe* (pp. 1–27). Cham: Palgrave Macmillan.

D'Amato, A. (2018). Risk-Taking in cooperative banks: Do board characteristics matter? *International Journal of Business and Social Science, 9*(11), 80–90.

Deville, A., & Lamarque, E. (2015). *Diversity of cooperative bank governance models questioning by regulation: An international qualitative research* (Group BPCE Working Paper, 1).

Di Salvo, R., & Lopez, J. S. (2010). The cooperative credit system in Italy. In *Cooperative banking in Europe* (pp. 148–162). London: Palgrave Macmillan.

Di Salvo, R., & Lopez, J. S. (2018). The reform of the cooperative banking sector in Italy. *New cooperative banking in Europe* (pp. 114–129). Cham: Palgrave Macmillan.

EACB. (2016). Corporate governance in co-operative banks. Key Features. Available on http://www.eacb.coop/en/home.html.

Ferri, G. (2012). *Credit cooperatives: Challenges and opportunities in the new global scenario* (Euricse Working Paper, N.031 | 12).

Groeneveld, H. M. (2014). Features, facts and figures of European cooperative banking groups over recent business cycles. *Journal of Entrepreneurial and Organizational Diversity, Special Issue on Cooperative Banks, 3*(1), 11–33.

International Cooperative Alliance, ICA, Official Web Site. https://www.ica.coop/en.

Italian Cooperative Credit, Official Web Site. http://www.creditocooperativo.it/.

Lamarque, E. (2018). The governance of cooperative banks: Main features and new challenges. In *New cooperative banking in Europe* (pp. 141–161). Cham: Palgrave Macmillan.

Mare, D. S., & Gramlich, D. (2020). Risk exposures of European cooperative banks: A comparative analysis. *Review of Quantitative Finance and Accounting*, 1–23. FORMATT.

Meyer, E. (2018). The new economic scenario and its impact on the cooperative banking business model. In *New cooperative banking in Europe* (pp. 29–45). Cham: Palgrave Macmillan.

Migliorelli, M. (2018). Cooperative banks lending during and after the great crisis. *New cooperative banking in Europe* (pp. 231–242). Cham: Palgrave Macmillan.

Ossola, G., Giovando, G., & Crovini, C. (2017). Cyber risk management in credit cooperative banks: A case study. In *10th Annual Conference of the EuroMed Academy of Business* (pp. 1239–1250). EuroMed Press.

Padoa-Schioppa, T. (1996, febbraio 22). Il credito cooperativo in Italia: realtà e problemi, *intervento al Convegno Sviluppo Economico e Intermediazione Finanziaria: Piccole imprese, Banche locali, Credito Cooperativo*. Roma.

Poli, F. (2019). The theoretical background of co-operative banking. In *Co-operative banking networks in Europe* (pp. 1–63). Cham: Palgrave Macmillan.

Sahut, J. M., & Bouheni, F. B. (2019). Profitability and risk-taking among cooperative banks in the Eurozone. *Economics Bulletin, 39*(2), 1103–1117.

Soana, M. G., & Ferri, G. (2019). Remuneration provisions, internal governance and risk taking in small cooperative banks. *International Journal of Business and Social Science, 10*(9).

Stefani, M. L., Vacca, V., Coin, D., Del Prete S., Demma, C., Galardo, M., ... Pellegrino, D. (2016). *Le banche locali e il finanziamento dei territori: evidenze per l'Italia (2007–2014)* (Banca d'Italia, Occasional Papers, n. 324).

CHAPTER 5

The Readiness of Cooperative Credit Banks in Knowledge Risk Management: Toward a Framework

Abstract In this chapter, the first Knowledge Risk Management framework specific for cooperative credit banks (CCBs) is proposed. To arrive at its composition, a case study on a sample of Italian CCBs was performed. A survey was conducted to verify the level of awareness of the banking staff regarding knowledge risks. The results highlighted a rather fragmented knowledge of knowledge risks, and the substantial lack of a precise KRM strategy within the CCBs analyzed. In this sense, the proposed framework could support banking management to fill the gaps in knowledge risks understanding, fostering a knowledge risk-aware culture in the bank.

Keywords Case study · Italian CCBs · KRM framework

5.1 Introduction

As previously stated, this book has a dual purpose: to contribute to the development of Knowledge Risk Management (KRM) strand, investigating the readiness of banks in knowledge risks, and to propose a KRM framework specific for banks. In particular, for cooperative credit banks. To achieve these goals, in this chapter, a case study to determine the awareness of bankers with respect to knowledge risks was conducted on

M. La Torre, *Risk in Banking*,
https://doi.org/10.1007/978-3-030-54498-0_5

a sample of Italian cooperative banks members of the *Federazione delle Banche di Credito Cooperativo dell'Abruzzo e del Molise (Fedam)*, and the first KRM framework was derived from data analysis, aimed at supporting banking management in contrasting the knowledge risks to which CCBs could be exposed.

For this purpose, the remainder of the present chapter is structured in the following way: Sects. 5.2–5.2.3 (and its sub-sections) deal with the different phases in which the case study is divided. In Sect. 5.3, case study's conclusions and implications are provided, which formed the basis for the proposal of a KRM framework specific for cooperative credit banks.

5.2 A Case Study to Investigate the Readiness of Cooperative Credit Banks in Knowledge Risks Management

5.2.1 Single-Case Study as Strategic Methodology

The choice of research methodology depends on the nature of the problem to be investigated and, consequently, the actual suitability of a method is connected to the nature of the phenomena to be explored (Noor, 2008). As anticipated above, in this Section, a case study is performed to investigate the readiness of cooperative credit banks (CCBs) in Knowledge Risk Management (KRM). Although this methodology has in some cases been attributed a lack of scientific rigor (Johnson, 1995), we believe is the most appropriate choice, as it is considered ideal for "revelatory cases where an observer may have access to a phenomenon that was previously inaccessible" (Tellis, 1997), and also because offering the possibility of adopting a real-time perspective rather than a retrospective one (Durst, Lindvall, & Bruns, 2018).

From a research point of view, Yin (2011, 2018), Merriam (1998) and Stake (1995) made the greatest contribution to case study research, providing scholars with procedures to follow for the use of this methodology (Yazan, 2015), and helping to overcome the common stereotype according to which case study is a method of last resort, suitable only for the exploratory phases of research, and just leading to unconfirmed conclusions (Yin, 1981).

With respect to these different contributions, we have chosen to follow Yin's methodological suggestions. According to the author, "case" is "generally a bounded entity (a person, organization, behavioral condition, event, or other social phenomenon), that serves as the main unit of analysis in a case study" (Yin, 2011, p. 6). This definition of "case" reflects author's advocacy for the case study as a legitimate empirical method of research, that "copes with the technically distinctive situation in which there will be many more variables of interest than data points; benefits from the prior development of theoretical propositions to guide design, data collection, and analysis; relies on multiple sources of evidence, with data needing to converge in a triangulating fashion" (Yin, 2018, p. 45). Case studies can take different compositional forms. Among categories of formats proposed by the author, in this work, the single-case study with a linear-analytic structure is employed. Therefore, the following Sections begin with issue or problem being studied, then proceed covering data collection, methodology, data analysis, findings, and ending with the conclusions and implications for the studied issue (Yin, 2018).

5.2.2 Conduct the Case Study

This case study is conducted with the aim of understanding whether cooperative credit banks are aware of knowledge risks, and whether strategies for their management are implemented. Thus, the research question is as follows:

How does cooperative credit banks (CCBs) handle Knowledge Risk Management?

The unit of analysis is a CCBs' Federation, made up of eight cooperative credit banks members, named *Federazione delle Banche di Credito Cooperativo dell'Abruzzo e del Molise (Fedam)*, located in central-southern Italy.

Italian cooperative credit is still currently under the effects of a recent reform that placed CCBs at complex challenges to play in maintaining high management and governance standards (see Chapter 4 of this work). Pure localism that has always distinguished these banks has had to integrate into a Cooperative Banking Group, which, while maintaining intact the distinctive characteristics of cooperative credit, such as mutuality, has led CCBs members to deal with important organizational changes in a more turbulent environment. In such a context, where human resources are required to adapt and manage relationships more complex than in the past, the possibility of being exposed to a series of risks linked to management of the knowledge necessary to face these changes is high. This situation, combined with the fact that, in general, KRM in banking and financial sector is a strand not yet fully developed (see Chapter 3 of this work), make the case study in question timely and necessary.

Data collection occurred between January and February 2020, and was carried out through a survey targeted at boards' directors and managers of cooperative banks belonging to the abovementioned Federation. Questionnaire has been designed to assess the awareness of KRM in the sample banks. For this reason, it was divided into sections, each addressing a topic: CCBs' risk management; how, in CCBs, knowledge is considered and managed; the awareness of risks related to knowledge use; the perception of the consequences of knowledge loss within the organization; as well as the effects of employee turnover on knowledge retention; and finally also possible strategies to deal with exposure to knowledge risks, in terms of actions to be taken and resources to be used in the bank. Questionnaires were sent through hard copy mail to CCBs, and 23 responses resulted.

The questionnaires sent back from the CCBs, and answers were analyzed using SPSS software. In the section below, the main results of the survey are presented.

5.2.3 *Analyze Case Study's Evidence*

Considering, at first, demographic matters, data showed respondents belonging to different genders, age groups, educational levels, and job positions, thus allowing to obtain opinions from different points of view. About gender and age group, for example, most of the respondents were male, while the age range was between 35 and 60. Respondents are mostly graduates, and have worked in the banking sector from a minimum of 10 years to a maximum of over 30 years (of which in many cases entirely in the CCBs analyzed), holding positions such as department manager, executive, and senior executive, distributed between traditional banking area, or credit area, or administration and finance, or management control, or marketing.

5.2.3.1 *CCBs' Risk Management*

About Risk Management, 63.6% of the participants claimed that in their organization the risk is associated with an eventuality of suffering damage connected to more or less foreseeable circumstances; 22.7% associated it with the possibility of an unexpected negative event; while less than 10% identified it with the possibility of an unexpected event not necessarily negative. To the question "how does your bank manage risk?", most of participants claimed that the bank relies especially on controls provided by regulation and, secondly, also on the implementation of human resources' knowledge. With respect to the major challenges facing banks after the crisis, the identification of a new mission, understood as a more advanced form of intermediation, was the response with more consensus; while being able to create principals inspired by the principle of proportionality, and therefore such as not to "plaster" bank's operations, was considered the main challenge facing the bank in the current regulation of banking system.

5.2.3.2 *CCBs' Knowledge Management*

More than 30% of respondents rated the effectiveness of information system of CCB in which they work as "somewhat ineffective," using a five-point scale (ranging from "extremely ineffective" to "effective"), motivating the response with the not always exploited possibility of implementing improvement plans even if easy to implement.

Going more specifically into Knowledge Management, 77.3% of the participants considered knowledge a resource of high value for the bank, recognizing it as a harbinger of benefits for the bank (45.5%), and greater skills for employee (27.3%). For this reason, Knowledge Management was widely recognized by respondents as an activity carried out within the bank which, in a static perspective, takes the form of an organizational system calibration that allows the correct positioning of human resources with specific skills, while in a dynamic perspective, in the realization of career paths consistent with a rational distribution of the operators' knowledge in relation to company needs.

5.2.3.3 *CCBs' Knowledge Risk Management*

Most of respondents claimed to know Knowledge Risk Management (57.1%), identifying it with the awareness of being able to make mistakes in the knowledge management process. Furthermore, given a list of the best-known knowledge risks with a summary of their main characteristics, the participants were asked to rate their perception of the probability that these risks may occur in their bank, using a scale from "frequent" (likely to occur regularly, two-thirds chance) to "improbable"(so unlikely it may not be experienced, less than one in ten chance); and to rate their perception of the consequences if these risks occurred at bank, using a scale from "catastrophic" (failure that would prevent the organization from meeting the primary operational requirements) to "minor" (failure would result in temporary degradation or loss of one or more capabilities within the organization).

The results highlighted how the risk of knowledge digitization turns out to be the option with the consequences considered worst for the bank if it presents itself, and was matched by the respondents with the highest probability of occurring among all the options present.

The knowledge hoarding risk was perceived by respondents as a potentially very dangerous knowledge risk for the bank, albeit associated with an average level of probability of being lower than the knowledge digitization risk. On the contrary, the knowledge spillover risk appears to be the option combined with the lower likelihood of going to the bank, but it is not considered a risk with dangerous consequences. The same is true for the risk of knowledge forgetfulness, which was combined with consequences of entities, but with a higher degree of likelihood than risk of knowledge spillover.

In any case, it is necessary to underline that for all the options in question the average degree of consequences is between 3 (major) and 4 (minor), that is, a relatively low degree on the scale from 1 (catastrophic) to 4 (minor).

To visualize the results of this section of survey, a positioning graph was created (Fig. 5.1).

5.2.3.4 *Knowledge Loss in CCBs*

To address risk of knowledge loss in CCBs, the questionnaire included a series of statements regarding hypothetical risky events (such as: decreased employee relationship between employees who stay and their bank; decreased morale for employees who stay; decreased productivity for employees who stay; decreased subject matter expertise; decreased experience; reduced capacity to innovate; reduced ability to pursue growth; reduced efficiency; provide competitors with an advantage; increased vulnerability to serious corporate risk) due to knowledge unavailability as a result of employee exit, or lost codified knowledge, or knowledge decay.

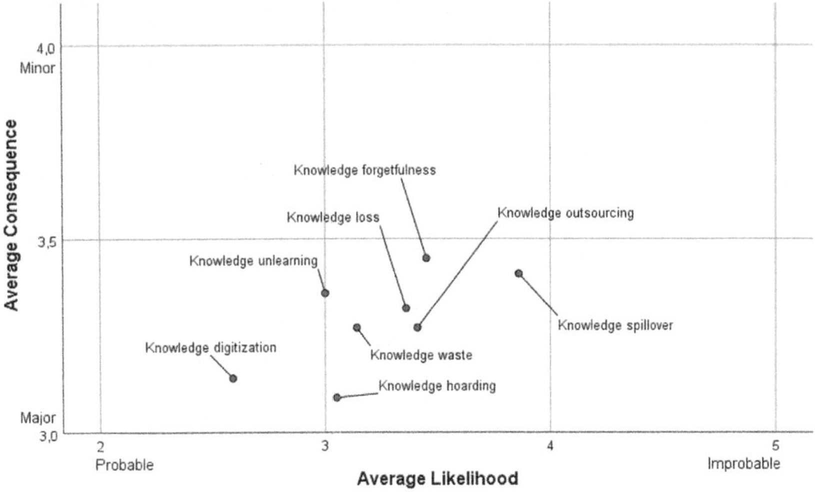

Fig. 5.1 Perceptions of knowledge risks (*Source* Our elaboration of the responses to the questionnaire using SPSS Software)

Participants were asked to rate their perception of the likelihood that such events may occur at their bank using a scale from "frequent" (likely to occur regularly, two-thirds chance) to "improbable"(so unlikely it may not be experienced, less than one in ten chance); and to rate their perception of the consequences if these risks occurred at bank, using a scale from "catastrophic" (failure that would prevent the organization from meeting the primary operational requirements) to "minor" (failure would result in temporary degradation or loss of one or more capabilities within the organization). Analyzing answers given by participants, it was found that almost all the options have an average degree of "consequences" around the value of 3 (or "major"); only the option "decreased employee relationship between employees who stay and their bank" had an average "consequences" score slightly higher than all the other options.

Instead, as regards the average likelihood, it was possible to note that the option considered by far the most remote was "provide competitors with an advantage," while the options are considered most likely were "decreased employee relationship between employees who stay and their bank" and "reduced ability to pursue growth." The possibility of a knowledge loss, therefore, was recognized as a potential threat regardless of

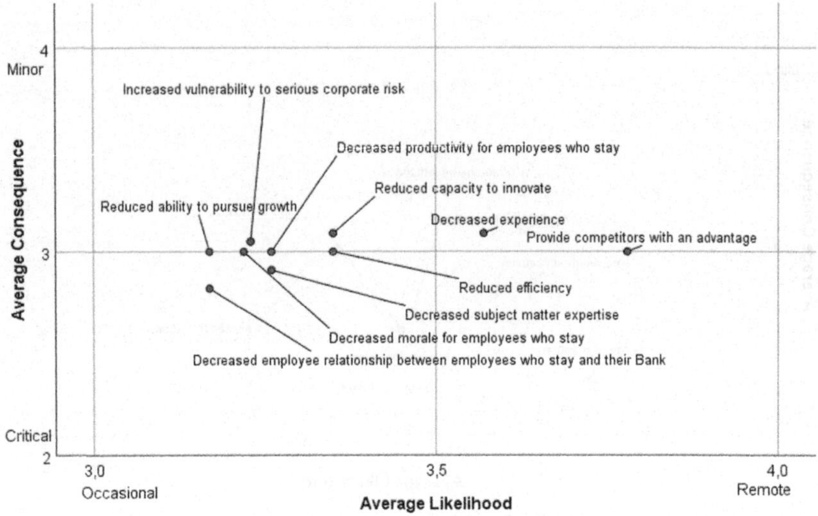

Fig. 5.2 Consequences of knowledge loss (*Source* Our elaboration of the responses to the questionnaire using SPSS Software)

what caused it, and the consequences in their opinion are directly reflected on the relationship between the employees who remain and the bank, as if to underline little confidence that governance can somehow make up for this loss, so much so that the difficulty in pursuing corporate growth objectives has also been identified as a probable consequence.

To visualize the results of this section of survey, a positioning graph was created (Fig. 5.2).

5.2.3.5 *Employee Turnover in CCBs*

This section of the survey focused on employee turnover and its possible consequences in terms of exposure to knowledge risks. In this case, participants were asked to reason about a series of hypothetical events following the exit of employees from the bank. In particular, these events referred to:

- when employees exit from the bank, they take their knowledge with them;

- when employees exit from the bank, employees who stay will decrease their knowledge;
- when employees exit from the bank, new employees who join will bring their new knowledge;
- when employees exit from the bank, the knowledge of employees who stay will increase in value.

Participants rated their perception of the likelihood of such events happening, using always the scale from "frequent" to "improbable," and their perception of impact on the bank of such events occurrence, using a scale from "very unimportant impact" to "very important impact." Results highlighted that respondents consider as events that could happen with greater probability and with the most significant impact on the bank the one according to which employees who leave the company take away their knowledge, and the one according to which remaining employees increase their knowledge value. In a sense, a sort of "self-compensation" of any post turnover loss of knowledge.

Instead, "employees who stay will decrease their knowledge" was the event believed to have a medium impact, but the most remote in terms of likelihood. Finally, "new employees who join will bring their new knowledge" turns out to be the option combined with the lowest impact between the various options, and a low intermediate of likelihood between the various events.

Also for results of this section of survey, a positioning graph was created (Fig. 5.3).

5.2.3.6 Risk Assessment in CCBs

At this point, the survey focused on risk assessment. In particular, the participants were asked to think about what consequences could arise if their work was not carried out according to the bank's expectations.

Most of the respondent employed in traditional banking and professional savings management, identified the loss of customers as a consequence of the performance of their work not according to the bank's expectations (35.3 and 33.3%). For financial and social security advisors, the loss of profit was the most indicated consequence of a possible inefficient performance of their work (respectively, 42.9 and 66.7%). Other consequences were indicated by the participants, albeit with lower percentages: reputational damage (23.5% according to those

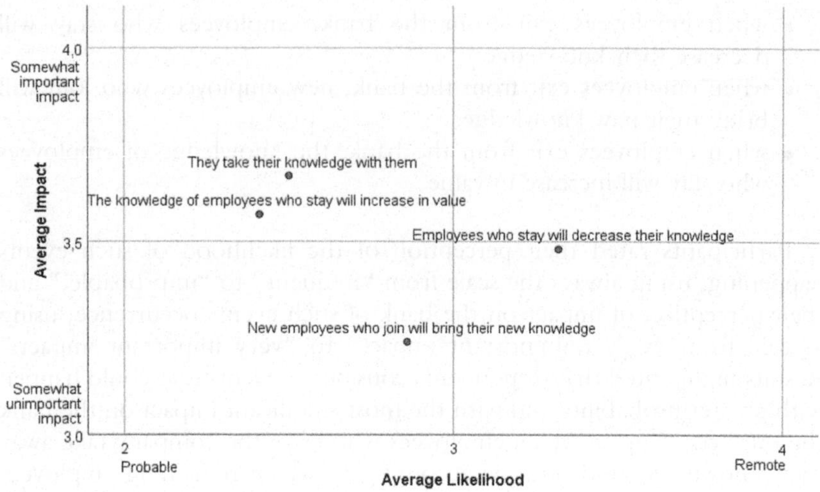

Fig. 5.3 Consequences of employee turnover (*Source* Our elaboration of the responses to the questionnaire using SPSS Software)

performing traditional banking; 14.3% according to financial consultants; 16.7% for insurance consultants); removal from office (14.3% according to financial advisors; 33.3% for pension advisors; 16.7% for insurance advisors); administrative irregularities (5.9% for those who carry out traditional banking); bank crisis (23.5% for those who carry out traditional banking); fundamental savings loss (16.7% according to professional savings managers); organizational disservices (according to all organizational consultants).

The respondents were further asked to rate their perception of the likelihood that the consequences above mentioned may occur at bank, using a scale from "frequent" to "improbable," and also to rate their perception of the impact in bank if those consequences occurred, using a scale from "catastrophic" to "minor."

The answers given highlighted how the "bank crisis" and "organizational inefficiencies" options were considered to be the most unlikely, but with the greatest impact on the bank, while "administrative irregularities" and "fundamental saving loss" were considered equally serious in terms of impact on the bank, but much higher, compared to the previous ones, in terms of probability.

In general, the option with the highest Likelihood ever turned out to be "civil/criminal cases," although it is considered not too impactful in the bank.

Finally, the consequence with the least degree both with reference to the probability of happening and with reference to the impact on the bank turned out to be "removal from office."

The positioning chart for this section of the survey is subsequently reported (Fig. 5.4).

Participants were also asked to think about possible knowledge resources which may minimize the risk events previously indicated as consequences of hypothetical inefficiencies in carrying out their work. They were then asked to indicate if there was a figure in their bank capable of managing knowledge resources necessary for the success of such strategies. Furthermore, they were asked what would happen if that figure were to leave the bank.

From the answers given, the following emerged.

In the case of profit loss, the knowledge resource indicated with the highest percentage (75%) was the training activity; for the reputational damage, the loss of customers and corporate crisis, in addition to the

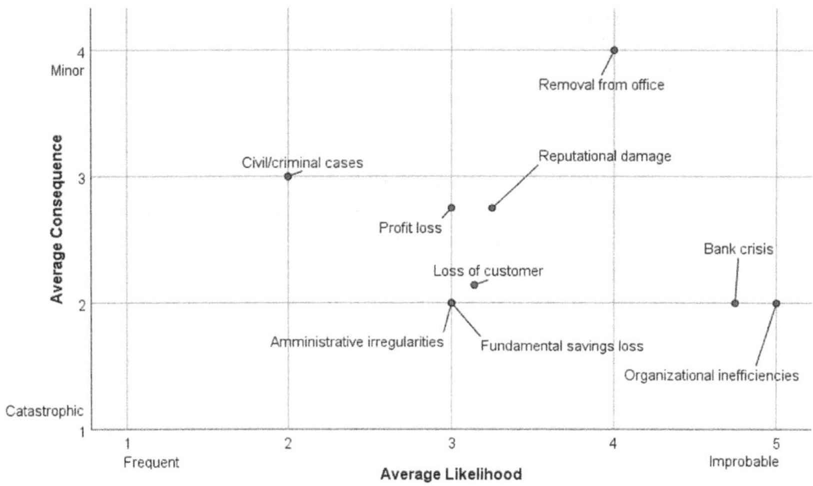

Fig. 5.4 Risky events. Likelihood and consequences (*Source* Our elaboration of the responses to the questionnaire using SPSS Software)

training activities, team working and coaching with experts were also mentioned; instead, simplification of IT processes was indicated as a knowledge resource in the event of a loss of fundamental savings.

With regard to the person indicated as capable of managing the knowledge resources just mentioned, the following emerged.

For training activities, 69.2% of respondents indicated the presence in the bank of a suitable person to manage it; Even the knowledge resource "coaching with expert," for 70% of the respondents, is covered by a subject within the bank, as well as for the "team work" resource; they do not believe that there is a person in the bank capable of managing the IT processes simplification.

In conclusion, when it was asked what would happen if the person in charge of managing knowledge resources left the bank, the participants replied as follows.

With reference to the training activity, coaching with expert and team working, most of respondents stated that the person in question would be replaced, and the work would be done satisfactorily (respectively, 38.5, 40, and 57.1%).

5.3 Develop Case Study's Conclusions and Implications: Toward a Knowledge Risk Management Framework Specific for Cooperative Credit Banks

The results of the survey reported above, strengthened in the author of this work, the belief that an effective KRM approach is particularly important for Italian cooperative credit banks, especially in the moment of profound changes they are going through.

In this section, a KRM framework is proposed with the aim of supporting banking management in identifying and managing knowledge risks which could arise from the increased complexity of their organizational structure, and due to consequent amount of new knowledge to manage.

According to a recent study on knowledge risk management in the public sector (Durst et al., 2018), we place the following assumptions at the base of this framework:

- In the CCBs analyzed, almost everyone recognizes the importance of knowledge as a useful resource for the competitiveness of the organization, but awareness of the risky side of this resource seems to be lacking.
- In the CCBs analyzed, there is lack of knowledge risk-aware culture. Management knows knowledge risks only in a formal way. There appears to be no planning and implementation of KRM strategy or activities.
- In the CCBs analyzed, there is the awareness that risky events may occur as a result of inefficiencies in the performance of work activities, but full awareness of the consequences that such events could have on the bank seems to be lacking.

CCBs' KRM framework is shown in Table 5.1

As can be seen from Table 5.1, the framework proposes a process that from the identification of potentially knowledge-risky situations leads to the identification of the knowledge resources not available for the bank, but necessary to manage a risky event. For each phase of this process, the actions to be taken to implement each phase and the subjects involved in the bank are identified.

The possible advantages of this framework essentially concern:

- it don't include too many activities. In this way, the performance of primary activities is not hindered, and space is left for the modulation and implementation of the framework at any time it is deemed appropriate/necessary;
- it is marked by "awareness." Each step and each activity of the process represents an invitation to think about knowledge risks and their harmfulness potential. In this way, all people within the organization are involved and informed, whether they have an active role in the process or not.

Table 5.1 CCBs' KRM framework

What	*How*	*Who*
Identification of potentially knowledge-risky situations	List the situations that: • put the bank in a position to manage new knowledge • place the bank in the need to find knowledge resources	Managers and employees equally involved (Produce an informative report about the phase outputs to be shared with all staff)
+		
Identification of bank activities potentially exposed to risky situations	List the activities that: • involve the creation of new knowledge • involve the sharing of knowledge • involve the outsourcing of knowledge	Managers and a select group of employees (Produce an informative report about the phase outputs to be shared with all staff)
=		
Identification of risky events	Reasoning about the enucleated activities and identifying those that can actually generate knowledge risks	Executives and managers (Produce an informative report about the phase outputs to be shared with all staff)
+		
Identification of available knowledge resources	On the basis of the activities identified as potentially generating knowledge risks, highlight the resources that the bank has available and which are deemed suitable to face these risks	Executives, managers and a special task force (Produce an informative report about the phase outputs to be shared with all staff)
=		
Identification of needed knowledge resources	List the risky events with which the available knowledge resources have failed and identify the most suitable knowledge resources but not yet available to the bank	Executives, managers and a special task force (possibly also external subjects) (Produce an informative report about the phase outputs to be shared with all staff)

Source Our elaboration

References

Durst, S., Lindvall, B., & Bruns, G. (2018). Knowledge risk management in the public sector: Insights into a Swedish municipality. *Journal of Knowledge Management, 24*(4), 717–735.

Johnson, D. (1995). Research methods in educational management. *British Journal of Educational Studies, 43*(2), 218–219.

Merriam, S. B. (1998). *Qualitative research and case study applications in education*. San Francisco, CA: Jossey-Bass.

Noor, K. B. M. (2008). Case study: A strategic research methodology. *American Journal of Applied Sciences, 5*(11), 1602–1604.

Stake, R. (1995). *The art of case research*. Newbury Park, CA: Sage.

Tellis, W. (1997). Application of a case study methodology. *The Qualitative Report, 3*(3), 1–19.

Yazan, B. (2015). Three approaches to case study methods in education: Yin, Merriam, and Stake. *The Qualitative Report, 20*(2), 134–152.

Yin, R. K. (1981). The case study as a serious research strategy. *Knowledge, 3*(1), 97–114.

Yin, R. K. (2011). *Applications of case study research*. Thousand Oaks: Sage.

Yin, R. K. (2018). *Case study research and applications* (6th ed.). Thousand Oaks: Sage.

CHAPTER 6

Conclusions

Abstract This chapter remarks on the main contents of the book. Specifically, some final reflections on the topics covered are included, in particular regarding motivations and beliefs that led the author to focus the analysis on Knowledge Risk Management (KRM) in the banking sector. Limitations and suggestions for future research, aimed at the implementation of an autonomous strand on KRM in banking and financial sectors, have been provided as well.

Keywords Knowledge Risk Management · Banks · Financial firms · Future research of KRM in banking and financial sectors

At the end of this work, some lessons have been learned. Much more remains to be learned.

First of all, the exploration of the field of Knowledge Risk Management (KRM) is still at an early stage and requires the commitment of scholars from all over the world dealing with different organizations, because KRM is an interface function that should be firmly anchored in any organizational structure, and should cover private and public organizations, small and large ones, as well as start-ups and mature companies (Durst & Henschel, 2020).

M. La Torre, *Risk in Banking*,
https://doi.org/10.1007/978-3-030-54498-0_6

Exactly this spirit guided the writing of the present book. (1) Wondering if banks and other financial firms could also benefit from the application of concepts, methodologies, and approaches deriving from KRM, and (2) if a study to verify the level of awareness of bank management about the existence of knowledge risks responded to the call for major contributions made by the precursors of the studies in this field. Considering the current situation of the global banking system, answers can only be affirmative.

Banks are still trying to rebuild the trust relationship with customers, but lessons from the past not seem to have been learned.

Despite mistakes made and the regulatory reform measures, some of the major global banks continued to reiterate dangerous behaviors such as inefficient management of complex "exotic" financial instruments, or the securitization of bad loans. Over ten years have passed since the global financial crisis, and there are still financial intermediaries fined by supervisors for various illegal behavior. Examples include Barclays and HSBC, respectively, for manipulating the reporting of interbank rates and financing of money laundering; and four Italian banks (Banca delle Marche, BancaEtruria, Cariferrara, Carichieti), because of the illegal conduct of their administrators.

Behaviors like these, and in general most of the banks' woes, seem to originate not only from inefficiencies in governance and management but, above all, from the lack of competence in risk management. And this lack of risk management competency persisted even after the global financial crisis. Banks would need longer-term and more deliberate, proactive, and sustainable solutions to develop their risk management expertise, rather than often ineffective short-term reactions (Koh, 2019).

One of these solutions could be to combine risk management and knowledge management activities. This integration of risk and knowledge management could bring greater advantages than standalone risk management; knowledge management activities allow, in fact, to seize resources made available by experts, and to promote the neutralization of knowledge on the web, the organization's repositories and past relationships, also allowing the formation of virtual risk management teams and virtual forums to share knowledge and experience. Definitely, the combination of these two management approaches turns organizations into learning environment (Rehman & Kifor, 2015).

Therefore, banks and other financial companies could rely on risk management implemented by the awareness that another category of risks can undermine the organization, i.e., knowledge risks. Thus, banking management may be able to understand that, for example, risk of knowledge loss could be as harmful as credit risk; that employee behavior such as knowledge hiding or knowledge hoarding could expose the bank to stress comparable to market risks' consequences; and also that risks such as knowledge unlearning or forgetfulness could compromise, for example, staff training courses; and risks such as knowledge waste could lead banks to reiterate the same mistakes that consecrated them as main responsible for the global financial crisis.

Bearing in mind the considerations expressed so far, a study investigating the readiness of banks for knowledge risks appeared to be timely, if not even necessary. In this book, a particular type of bank is considered, namely, the Italian cooperative credit banks (CCBs). This choice was made due to the particular period of changes that Italian cooperative credit faced in recent years. The recent reform of the Italian cooperative banking sector, in fact, imposed on the participating CCBs a reorganization into a banking group, while maintaining their distinctive character of local bank. This organizational transformation implied an increasingly complex knowledge to manage and, consequently, the greater possibility of exposure to knowledge risks for the banks.

The results of the analysis conducted partially demonstrated this. In fact, even if the CCBs'employees seemed to have knowledge, at least notional, of knowledge risks, there is still no real awareness in banking management of their potential harmfulness. On the basis of this, a framework to start approaching knowledge risk management has been proposed, with the awareness that it is only the first step of a path that must be subsequently completed and implemented over time.

The proposed framework is focused on the process that from the identification of potentially knowledge-risky situations leads to the identification of the knowledge resources not available for the bank, but necessary to manage a risky event. This should encourage the formation of a knowledge risk-aware culture in banking staff. For this purpose, each step and each activity of the proposed framework were structured so that represented an invitation to think about knowledge risks and their harmfulness potential. In this way, all people within the organization are involved and informed, whether they have an active role in this process or not.

This research presents limitations that mainly concern the small size of the sample used in the analysis. This does not allow to generalize the findings, but could represent anyway a starting point for future research on KRM in the banking and financial sectors. In this regard, important avenues for future research come from a work on KRM already mentioned several times in this book (Durst & Henschel, 2020). Among these suggestions, what we think could be particularly useful for future developments of a specific KRM strand for banks and other financial companies, is the one that poses the following questions (Durst & Henschel, 2020, p. 257):

- How to disseminate the awareness about risks and their management among all organization members?
- How to develop a risk-aware mindset in different types of organizations?
- How to develop a risk-aware culture in different types of organizations?
- How to develop and execute KRM-related training programs?
- Who should be in charge of running these programs?

It is time to answer these questions.

References

Durst, S., & Henschel, T. (2020). *Knowledge risk management: From theory to praxis*. Berlin: Springer.

Koh, E. H. (2019). *Risk management competency development in banks: An integrated approach*. Berlin: Springer.

Rehman, Z., & Kifor, C. (2015). Risk management in perspective of knowledge management a brief survey. *ACTA Universitatis Cibiniensis*, 67(1).

Index

M. La Torre, *Risk in Banking*,
https://doi.org/10.1007/978-3-030-54498-0

The manufacturer's authorised representative in the EU is Springer Nature Customer Service Centre GmbH, Europaplatz 3, 69115 Heidelberg, Germany. If you have any concerns regarding our products, please contact ProductSafety@springernature.com

Printed and bound by CPI Group (UK) Ltd, Croydon, CR0 4YY
30/09/2026
02225514-0004